Ten-Tronck's Millionaire Directory

Ten-Tronck's Millionaire Directory

Published by:

 Axiom Information Resources

Ann Arbor, Michigan 48107

Millionaire Directory
Published by Axiom Information Resources
Ann Arbor, Michigan 48107 USA

Copyright © 2003 Axiom Information Resources

All rights reserved. No part of this publication
may be reproduced or distributed in any form or
by any means, or stored in a data base or retrieval
system, without the prior written permission of
the publishers.

Published by:
Axiom Information Resources
P.O. Box 8015
Ann Arbor, MI 48107

Printed in USA
ISBN # 0-943213-46-0

Cover Design by: Concialdi Design

SPECIAL SALES
The Millioanire Directory is
available at special quantity discounts
for bulk purchases. For information write:

Axiom Information Resources
P.O. Box 8015-TMD
Ann Arbor, MI 48107

INTRODUCTION

Welcome to the 2nd edition of the Millionaire Directory. The objective of this Directory is to provide the most accurate and up-to-date addresses of millionaires. This new edition incorporates many addresses that are not included in our previous edition. It's more than just a tool for the curious, the people who want to know who are the wealthy elites, what they do and where to contact them. This Directory is also an invaluable resource tool for the reference librarian, fund-raiser, or anyone with any reason to contact a person who is extremely wealthy.

The editors have researched and arranged names and addresses on thousands of millionaires, they are engaged in all fields of occupations. If a person is a millionaire, it is our objective to find his or her name and address and list it in the Millionaire Directory.

Most millionaire welcome correspondence concerning their lives and accomplishments as well as give advice and tips on how to become successful and wealthy like they have. However, when writing to a person who is rich, as well as writing to Axiom Information Resources Inc. remember, for convenience sake, it is always best to enclose a stamped, self-addressed envelope. Of course, the editorial staff and publisher cannot guarantee that listed millionaires will respond to correspondence.

Also note that this directory is not a mailing list and shall not be considered as such, due the length of time it takes to gather and publish this book inaccuracies are inevitable. Nevertheless we have made every effort possible to ensure that the information contained in the Millionaire Directory is up-to-date and accurate as possible. We also cannot accept responsibility for inaccuracies created by a listed person moving or changing his or her mail arrangements after the directory went to press.

We welcome any suggestions or inquiries concerning the Millionaire Directory, and we sincerely hope this expanded edition will provide our readers with the necessary information to accomplish all targeted objectives. All inquiries concerning this book should be sent to Axiom Information Resources, Inc., P.O. Box 8015-Millions, Ann Arbor, Michigan 48107 U.S.A.
You may also visit us at our web site: http://www.celebritylocator.com.

Millionaire Directory 2nd edition

A

Robert B. Abbott
525 University Avenue, Suite 800
Palo Alto, CA 94301
"Business-Venture Capitalist"

Richard A. Abdoo
P.O. Box 2949
Milwaukee, WI 53201
"Business-(CEO) Wisconsin Energy"

John E. Abele
One Boston Scientific Place
Natick, MA 01760
"Business-Medical Devices"

Daniel S. Abraham
P.O. Box 3625
West Palm Beach, FL 33402
"Business-Slim Fast"

Leonard Abramson
1425 Horsham Road
North Wales, PA 19454
"Business-U.S. Heathcare"

F. Duane Ackerman
1155 Peachtree Street NE
Atlanta, GA 30309
"Business-(CEO) Bell South"

K. S. (Bud) Adams, Jr
4400 Post Oak Parkway
Houston, TX 77027
"Business-(CEO) Adams Resources & Energy"

Marty E. Adams
P.O. Box 428
Bowling Green, OH 43402
"Business (CEO) Sky Financial Group"

Richard M. Adams
P.O. Box 1508
Parkersburg, WV 26101
"Business-(CEO) United Bankshares"

Terence Adderley
999 West Big Beaver Road
Troy, MI 48084
"Business-(CEO) Kelly Services"

Sheldon Adelson
3355 Las Vegas Blvd. South
Las Vegas, NV 89109
"Business-Venetian Hotel & Caniso"

Rahul Aggarwal
11150 Santa Monica Blvd. Suite 1200
Los Angeles, CA 90025
"Business-Venture Capitalist"

Hassan Ahmed
5 Carlisle Road
Westford, MA 01886
"Business-(CEO) Sonus Networks"

Daniel F. Akerson
1505 Farm Credit Drive
McLean, VA 22102
"Business-(CEO) XO Communications"

Tom A. Alberg
1000 Second Ave., Ste. 3700
Seattle, WA 98104
"Business-Venture Capitalist"

Bruce Albertson
1821 West Iomega Way
Roy, UT 84067
"Business-(CEO) Iomega"

William Aldinger III
2700 Sanders Road
Prospect Heights, IL 60070
"Business-(CEO) Household International"

Millionaire Directory 2nd edition

Kobi Alexander
170 Crossways Park Drive
Woodbury, NY 11797
"Business-(CEO) Comverse Technology"

Paul Allaire
P.O. Box 1600
Stamford, CT 06904
"Business-(CEO) Xerox"

Robert Allbritton
1503 Pennsylvania Avenue NW
Washington, DC 20005
"Business-(CEO) Riggs National"

Herbert A. Allen
711 - 5th Avenue, 9th Floor
New York, NY 10022
"Business-Allen & Co., Investments"

Paul Gardner Allen
110 - 100th Avenue NE, Suite 550
Bellevue, WA 98004
"Business-Software (Microsoft)"

John A. Allison IV
200 West Second Street
Winston-Salem, NC 27101
"Business-(CEO) BB&T"

Robert Allison Jr
P.O. Box 1330
Houston, TX 77251
"Business-(CEO) Anadarko Petroleum"

Richard J. Almeida
500 West Monroe Street
Chicago, IL 60661
"Business-(CEO) Heller Financial"

Derek Lemke-von Ammon
c/o Thomas Weisel partners
1 Montgomery Street
San Francisco, CA 94104
"Business-Venture Capitalist"

Daniel Amos
1932 Wynnton Road
Columbus, GA 31999
"Business-(CEO) Aflac"

Donald H. Anderson
P.O. Box 5660
Denver, CO 80217
"Business-(CEO) TransMontaigne"

Edward T. Anderson
950 Winter St., Ste. 4600
Waltham, MA 02451
"Business-Venture Capitalist"

Jim Anderson
70 Willow Rd, Suite 200
Menlo Park, CA 94025
"Business-Venture Capitalist"

John Edward Anderson
401 South Anderson Street
Los Angeles, CA 90033
"Business-Beverage"

Mark A. Anderson
520 Main Avenue
Fargo, ND 58124
"Business-(CEO) Community First Bankshares"

Richard Anderson
5101 Northwest Drive
St Paul, MN 55111
"Business-(CEO) Northwest Airlines"

G. Allen Andreas
4666 Faries Parkway
Dacatur, IL 62525
"Business-(CEO) Archer Daniels"

Andrew L. Anker
2480 Sand Hill Road, Suite 101
Menlo Park, CA 94025
"Business-Venture Capitalist"

Millionaire Directory   2nd edition

Walter H. Annenberg
St. Davis Center, Suite A-200
150 Radnor - Chester Road
St. Davis, PA 19087
"Business-Publishing"

Philip F. Anschutz
1801 California Street
Denver, CO 80202
"Business-Qwest Communications"

Mary Anselmo
6560 Rock Spring Drive
Bethesda, MD 20817
"Business-Comsat Corp."

Steven R. Appleton
P.O. Box 6
Boise, ID 83707
"Business-CEO (Micron Technology)"

Joe Aragona
701 N. Brazos St., Suite 1400
Austin, Texas 78701
"Business-Venture Capitalist"

Nolan D. Archibald
701 East Joppa Road
Towson, MD 21286
"Business-(CEO) Black & Decker"

Juan Arenado
P.O. Box 362589
San Juan, PR 00936
"Business-(CEO) Santander BanCorp"

George Leon Argyros
949 South Coast Drive #600
Costa Mesa, CA 92626
"Business-Real Estate"

Micky Arison
3655 N.W. 87th Avenue
Miami, FL 33178
"Business-Carnival Cruise Lines"

C. Michael Armstrong
c/o AT&T Corp.
295 N. Maple Avenue
Basking Ridge, NJ 07920
"Business-(CEO) AT&T"

Greg L. Armstrong
500 Dallas Street
Houston, TX 77002
"Business-(CEO) Plains Resources"

Jeffrey T. Arnold
3399 Peachtree Road NE
Atlanta, GA 30326
"Business-(CEO) WebMD"

David Aronoff
880 Winter Street
Waltham, MA 02451
"Business-Venture Capitalist"

John Arrillaga
2560 Mission College Blvd. Suite #101
Santa Clara, CA 95054
"Business-Real Estate"

Brian Ascher
2494 Sand Hill Road, Suite 200
Menlo Park, CA 94025
"Business-Venture Capitalist"

Alan Austin
428 University Avenue
Palo Alto, CA 94301
"Business-Venture Capitalist"

Ramani Ayer
Hartford Plaza
Hartford, CT 06115
"Business- (CEO) Hartford Financial"

Millionaire Directory   2nd edition

Stephen Bachmann
950 Tower Lane, 18th Floor
Foster City, CA 94404
"Business-Venture Capitalist"

Robert Bagby
One North Jefferson Avenue
St Louis, MO 63103
"Business-(CEO) AG Edwards"

James Bagley
4650 Cushing Parkway
Fremont, CA 94538
"Business-(CEO) Lam Research"

Shanda Bahles
2884 Sand Hill Road, Suite121
Menlo Park, CA 94025
"Business-Venture Capitalist"

Keith E. Bailey
P.O. Box 2400
Tulsa, OK 74172
"Business-(CEO) William Companies"

Robert L. Bailey
3975 Freedom Circle
Santa Clara, CA 95054
"Business-(CEO) PMC-Sierra"

Thomas Bailey
P.O. Box 173375
Denver, CO 80217
"Business-Investments"

G. Thomas Baker
P.O. Box 10580
Reno, NV 89510
"Business-(CEO) Int'l Game Technology"

George R. Baker
5 Hanover Square
New York, NY 10004
"Business-(CEO) Reliance Group"

Leslie M. Baker, Jr
P.O. Box 3099
Winston-Salem, NC 27150
"Business-(CEO) Wachovia"

Dennis Bakke
1001 North 19th Street
Arlington, VA 22209
"Business-(CEO) AES"

Alex Balkanski
2480 Sand Hill Rd., Suite 200
Menlo Park, CA 94025
"Business-Venture Capitalist"

Steven A. Ballmer
One Microsoft Way
Redmond, WA 98052
"Business-(CEO) Microsoft"

Diosdado Banatao
635 Waverley Street
Palo Alto, CA 94301
"Business-Venture Capitalist"

Jeffrey C. Barbakow
3820 State Street
Santa Barbara, CA 93105
"Business-(CEO) Tenet Healthcare"

James Barksdale
2730 Sand Hill Road
Menlo Park, CA 94025
"Business-Netscape & Venture Capitalist"

Edward Barnholt
395 Page Mill Road
Palo Alto, CA 94306
"Business-(CEO) Agilent Technologies"

Millionaire Directory   2nd edition

William M. Barnum, Jr.
11150 Santa Monica Blvd. Suite 1200
Los Angeles, CA 90025
"Business-Venture Capitalist"

J. James Barr
P.O. Box 1770
Voorhees, NJ 08043
"Business-(CEO) American Water Works"

Craig Barrett
2200 Mission College Blvd.
Santa Clara, CA 95052
"Business-(CEO) Intel"

Michael Barrington
801 Cherry Street
Fort Worth, TX 76102
"Business-(CEO) AmeriCredit"

Peter Barris
One Freedom Square
11951 Freedom Drive, Suite 1240
Reston, VA 20190
"Business-Venture Capitalist"

Timothy Barrows
Bay Colony Corporate Center
1000 Winter St., Suite 4500
Waltham, MA 02451
"Business-Venture Capitalist"

Glen A. Barton
100 North East Adams Street
Peoria, IL 61629
"Business-(CEO) Caterpillar"

Forest Baskett
2490 Sand Hill Road
Menlo Park, CA 94025
"Business-Venture Capitalist"

Lee Marshall Bass
201 Main Street
Fort Worth, TX 76102
"Business-Investments & Oil"

Perry Richardson Bass
201 Main Street
Fort Worth, TX 76102
"Business-Investments & Oil"

Robert Muse Bass
P.O. Box 803546
Dallas, TX 75380
"Business-Investments & Oil"

Frank Batten
150 W. Brambleton Avenue
Norkford, VA 23510
"Business-Media, Publishing"

J. T. Battenberg III
5725 Delphi Drive
Troy, MI 48098
"Business-(CEO) Delphi Automotive Sys."

Charles T. Bauer
11 Greenway Plaza #100
Houston, TX 77047
"Business-Money Manager"

Stephen Baum
101 Ash Street
San Diego, CA 92101
"Business-(CEO) Sempra Energy"

Robert Beauchamp
2101 Citywest Blvd.
Houston, TX 77042
"Business-(CEO) BMC Software"

Riley P. Bechtel
50 Beale Street
San Francisco, CA 94105
"Business-Construction"

Stephen Davidson Bechtel, Jr.
50 Beale Street
San Francisco, CA 94105
"Business-Construction"

Millionaire Directory   2nd edition

Douglas Becker
1000 Lancaster Street
Baltimore, MD 21202
"Business-(CEO) Sylvan Learning Systems"

Charles Beeler
2884 Sand Hill Road, Suite 121
Menlo Park, CA 94025
"Business-Venture Capitalist"

Peter Behrendt
2490 Sand Hill Road
Menlo Park, CA 94025
"Business-Venture Capitalist"

Bay Colony Corporate Center
1000 Winter St., Suite 4500
Waltham, MA 02451
"Business-Venture Capitalist"

David Beirne
2480 Sand Hill Rd., Suite 200
Menlo Park, CA 94025
"Business-Venture Capitalist"

Alain J Belda
201 Isabella Street
Pittsburgh, PA 15212
"Business-(CEO) Alcoa"

Robert Benmosche
One Madison Avenue
New York, NY 10010
"Business-(CEO) MetLife"

Jeffrey S. Bennett
11150 Santa Monica Blvd. Suite 1200
Los Angeles, CA 90025
"Business-Venture Capitalist"

Robert R. Bennett
9197 South Peoria Street
Englewood, CO 80112
"Business-(CEO) AT&T Liberty Media"

Stephen Bennett
2535 Garcia Avenue
Mountain View, CA 94043
"Business-(CEO) Intuit"

William Gordon Bennett
2535 Las Vegas Blvd South
Las Vegas, NV 89109
"Business-Hotel & Casino"

Carl Edwin Berg
10050 Bandley Drive
Cupertino, CA 95014
"Business-Investments & Oil"

Jim Berglund
2223 Avenida de la Playa, Suite 300
La Jolla, CA 92037
"Business-Venture Capitalist"

William R. Berkley
P.O. Box 2518
Greenwich, CT 06836
"Business-(CEO) WR Berkley"

Timothy Barrows
Bay Colony Corporate Center
1000 Winter St., Suite 4500
Waltham, MA 02451
"Business-Venture Capitalist"

Douglas A. Berthiaume
34 Maple Street
Milford, MA 01757
"Business-(CEO) Waters"

Kurt L. Betcher
525 University Avenue, Suite 800
Palo Alto, CA 94301
"Business-Venture Capitalist"

Gordon M. Bethune
P.O. Box 4607
Houston, TX 77210
"Business-(CEO) Continental Airlines"

Millionaire Directory   2nd edition

Jeffrey P. Bezos
P.O. Box 81226
Seattle, WA 98108
"Business-(CEO) Amazon.com"

Aneel Bhusri
2929 Campus Dr., Suite 400
San Mateo, CA 94403
"Business-Venture Capitalist"

Geoffrey Bible
120 Park Avenue
New York, NY 10017
"Business-(CEO) Philip Morris"

H. Raymond Bingham
2655 Sealy Avenue
San Jose, CA 95134
"Business-(CEO) Cadence Design"

Stephen J. Bisciotti
6992 Columbia Gateway Drive
Columbia, MD 21046
"Business-Staffing Services"

W. Louis Bissette III
11150 Santa Monica Blvd. Suite 1200
Los Angeles, CA 90025
"Business-Venture Capitalist"

David Black
1 Gorham Island
Westport, CT 06880
"Business-Venture Capitalist"

Norman P. Blake, Jr.
6111 North River Road
Rosemont, IL 60018
"Business-(CEO) Comdisco"

James H. Blanchard
P.O. Box 120
Columbus, GA 31902
"Business-(CEO) Synovus Financial"

Authur M. Blank
3290 Northside Pkwy., NW, #600
Atlanta, GA 30327
"Business-Home Depot"

Jeffrey L. Bleustein
3700 West Juneau Avenue
Milwaukee, WI 53208
"Business-(CEO) Harley-Davidson"

Gary Bloom
1600 Plymouth Street
Mountain View, CA 94043
"Business-(CEO) Veritas Software"

Peter L. Bloom
c/o General Atlantic Partners
Three Pickwick Plaza
Greenwich, CT 06830
"Business-Venture Capitalist"

Michael Ruben Bloomberg
City Hall
New York, NY 10007
"Business-Financial News"

Neil Gary Bluhm
900 North Michigan Avenue # 1100
Chicago, IL 60611
"Business-Real Estate"

John Blystone
P.O. Box 3301
Muskegon, MI 49443
"Business-(CEO) SPX"

Robert H. Bohannon
1850 North Central Avenue
Phoenix, AZ 85077
"Business-(CEO) Viad"

Robert Bolinger
26 North Cedar Street
Lititz, PA 17543
"Business-(CEO) Susquehanna Bancshares"

Millionaire Directory   2nd edition

Stephen F. Bollenbach
9336 Civic Center Drive
Beverly Hills, CA 90210
"Business-(CEO) Hilton Hotels"

Frank Bonsal
1119 St. Paul Street
Baltimore, MD 21202
"Business-Venture Capitalist"

Michael Bonsignore
101 Columbia Road
Morristown, NJ 07960
"Business-(CEO) Honeywell"

Franklin Otis Booth, Jr.
P.O. Box 1000
Lebec, CA 93243
"Business-Investments"

Jon Boscia
1500 Market Street
Philadelphia, PA 19102
"Business-(CEO) Lincoln National"

Amar Gopal Bose
The Mountain
Framington, MA 01701
"Business-Bose Sound Systems"

Jack Bovender, Jr
One Park Plaza
Nashville, TN 37203
"Business-(CEO) HCA-The Healthcare Co."

J. Herbert Boydstun
P.O. Box 61540
New Orleans, LA 70161
"Business-(CEO) Hibernia"

Donald L. Bren
550 Newport Center Drive
Newport Beach, CA 92660
"Business-Real Estate"

Leland Brendsel
8200 Jones Branch Drive
McLean, VA 22102
"Business-(CEO) Freddie Mac"

Jim Breyer
428 University Avenue
Palo Alto, CA 94301
"Business-Venture Capitalist"

William Bricker
200 Public Square
Cleveland, OH 44114
"Business-(CEO) LTV"

Eli Broad
Sun America Center
Los Angeles, CA 90067
"Business-Investments"

James Broadhead
P.O. Box 1400
Juno Beach, FL 33408
"Business-(CEO) FPL Group"

Jeffrey D. Brody
3000 Sand Hill Rd., Bldg. 2, Suite 290
Menlo Park, CA 94025
"Business-(CEO) RedPoint Ventures"

Edgar Bronfman, Jr.
31122 Broad Beach Road
Malibu, CA 90265
"Business-Liquor"

Edgar Bronfman, Sr.
375 Park Avenue
New York, NY 10152
"Business-Liquor"

Mike Brooks
30 Rockefeller Plaza, Room 5508
New York, NY 10112
"Business-Venture Capitalist"

Millionaire Directory   2nd edition

Roger K. Brooks
699 Walnut Street
Des Moines, IA 50309
"Business-(CEO) AmerUs Group"

Steven Brooks
950 Tower Lane, 18th Floor
Foster City, CA 94404
"Business-Venture Capitalist"

Todd Brooks
2800 Sand Hill Road, Suite 250
Menlo Park, CA 94025
"Business-Venture Capitalist"

John W. Brown
2527 Fairfield Road
Portage, MI 49002
Business-(CEO) Stryker"

Joseph W. Brown, Jr
113 King Street
Armonk, NY 10504
"Business-(CEO) MBIA"

Owsley Brown II
P.O. Box 1080
Louisville, KY 40201
"Business-(CEO) Brown-Forman"

Richard Brown
5400 Legacy Drive
Plano, TX 75024
"Business-(CEO) EDS"

Wayne H. Brunetti
414 Nicollet Mall
Minneapolis, MN 55402
"Business-(CEO) Xcel Energy"

John E. Bryson
P.O. Box 999
Rosemead, CA 91770
"Business-(CEO) Edison International"

George Buckley
1 North Field Court
Lake Forest, IL 60045
"Business-(CEO) Brunswick"

Warren Edward Buffett
1440 Kiewit Plaza
Omaha, NE 68131
"Business-(CEO) Berkshire Hathaway"

Steven A. Burd
5918 Stoneridge Mall Road
Pleasanton, CA 94588
"Business-(CEO) Safeway"

H Peter Burg
76 South Main Street
Akron, OH 44308
"Business-(CEO) FirstEnergy"

Robert Burgess
33 Bloomfield Hills Parkway
Bloomfield Hills, MI 48304-2946
"Business-(CEO) Pulte"

William T. Burgin
83 Walnut Street
Wellesley Hills, MA 02481
"Business-Venture Capitalist"

Ronald Burkle
1550 Redwood Road
Salt Lake City, UT 84104
"Business-Supermarkets"

David A. Burner
Four Coliseum Centre
Charlotte, NC 28217
"Business-(CEO) BF Goodrich"

Kennett Burnes
Two Seaport Lane
Boston, MA 02210
"Business-(CEO) Cabot"

Millionaire Directory   2nd edition

Daniel P. Burnham
141 Spring Street
Lexington, MA 02421
"Business-(CEO) Raytheon"

Robert N. Burt
200 East Randolph Drive
Chicago, IL 60601
"Business-(CEO) FMC"

August Busch III
One Busch Place
St Louis, MO 63118
"Business-(CEO Anheuser-Bush, Beer"

Charles C. Butt
646 Main Avenue
San Antonio, TX 78204
"Business-Grocery Stores"

Brook Byers
2750 Sand Hill Road
Menlo Park, CA 94025
Business-Investments (KPCB)

Vincent A. Calarco
One American Lane
Greenwich, CT 06831
"Business-(CEO) Crompton"

Lawrence V. Calcano
c/o Goldman Sachs
85 Broad St.
New York, NY 10004
"Business-Banker"

Lewis Campbell
40 Westminster Street
Providence, RI 02903
"Business-(CEO) Textron"

Michael Capellas
P.O. Box 692000
Houston, TX 77269
"Business-(CEO) Compaq Computers"

Thos E. Capps
P.O. Box 26532
Richmond, VA 23261
Business-(CEO) Dominion Resources"

Bandel Carano
525 University Avenue, Suite 1300
Palo Alto, CA 94301
"Business-Venture Capitalist"

James R. Cargill
P.O. Box 5697
Minneapolis, MN 55440
"Business-Cargill Inc."

LeRoy T. Carlson, Jr
30 North LaSalle Street
Chicago, IL 60602
"Business-(CEO) Tele & Data Systems"

Daniel A. Carp
343 State Street
Rochester, NY 14650
"Business-(CEO) Eastman Kodak"

Richard L. Carrion
P.O. Box 362708
San Juan, PR 00936
"Business-(CEO) Popular"

Philip Carroll, Jr
One Enterprise Drive
Aliso Viejo, CA 92656
"Business-(CEO) Fluor"

Peter Cartwright
50 West San Fernando Street
San Jose, CA 95113
"Business-(CEO) Calpine"

Millionaire Directory   2nd edition

Donald J. Carty
P.O. Box 619616
DFW Airport, TX 75261
"Business-(CEO) AMR"

Steve Case
22000 AOL Way
Dulles, VA 20166
"Business-AOL Founder"

Joe Casey
One Canal Park, Suite 1120
Cambridge, MA 02142
"Business-Venture Capitalist"

Robert G. Catell
One MetroTech Center
Brooklyn, NY 11201
"Business-(CEO) KeySpan"

Frank Caufield
2750 Sand Hill Road
Menlo Park, CA 94025
Business-Investments (KPCB)

William Cavanaugh III
P.O. Box 1551
Raleigh, NC 27602
"Business-(CEO) Progress Energy"

James Cayne
245 Park Avenue
New York, NY 10167
"Business-(CEO) Bear Stern Companies"

Ted T. Cecala
1100 North Market Street
Wilmington, DE 19890
"Business-(CEO) Wilmington Trust"

Nicholas Chabraja
3190 Fairview Park Drive
Falls Church, VA 22042
"Business-(CEO) General Dynamics"

Malcolm Green Chace
P.O. Box 9488
Providence, RI 02940
"Business-Investments"

Paul Chamberlain
1585 Broadway
New York, NY 10036
"Business-Morgan Stanley Banker"

John T. Chambers
170 West Tasman Drive
San Jose, CA 95134
"Business-(CEO) Cisco Systems"

George W. Chamillard
321 Harrison Avenue
Boston, MA 02118
"Business- (CEO) Teradyne"

J. Harold Chandler
2211 Congress Street
Portland, ME 04122
"Business-(CEO) UnumProvident"

Rob S. Chandra
535 Middlefield Road, Suite 245
Menlo Park, CA 94025
"Business-Venture Capitalist"

Allen Chao
311 Bonnie Circle
Corona, CA 92882
"Business-(CEO) Watson Pharmaceuticals"

Rob Chaplinsky
2775 Sand Hill Road, Suite 240
Menlo Park, CA 94025
"Business-Venture Capitalist"

Thomas F. Chapman
1550 Peachtree Street NW
Atlanta, GA 30309
"Business-(CEO) Equifax"

Millionaire Directory 2nd edition

Paul R. Charron
1441 Broadway
New York, NY 10018
"Business-(CEO) Liz Claiborne"

Paul W. Chellgren
P.O. Box 391
Covington, KY 41012
"Business-(CEO) Ashland Gas & Oil"

Wu-Fu Chen
c/o Acorn Campus
6 Results Way
Cupertino, CA 95014
"Business-(CEO) Acorn Campus"

Kenneth Chenault
World Financial Center
New York, NY 10285
"Business-(CEO) American Express"

Charles Chi
2929 Campus Dr., Suite 400
San Mateo, CA 94403
"Business-Venture Capitalist"

Bruce Chizen
345 Park Avenue
San Jose, CA 95110
"Business-(CEO) Adobe Systems"

Anthony U. Choe
11150 Santa Monica Blvd. Suite 1200
Los Angeles, CA 90025
"Business-Venture Capitalist"

Jeffrey Christian
5825 Science Park Dr., Suite 400
Cleveland, OH 44122
"Business-(CEO) Christian & Timbers"

Jerry Christopher
83 Walnut Street
Wellesley Hills, MA 02481
"Business-Venture Capitalist"

Bruce Claflin
5400 Bayfront Plaza
Santa Clara, CA 95052
"Business-(CEO) 3Com"

Tom Clancy
2223 Avenida de la Playa, Suite 300
La Jolla, CA 92037
"Business-Venture Capitalist"

James H. Clarke
669 River Drive, Center 2
Elmwood park, NJ 07407
"Business-Netscape co-founder"

Robert F. Clarke
P.O. Box 730
Honolulu, HI 96808
"Business-(CEO) Hawaiian Electric"

Robert S. Cline
P.O. Box 662
Seattle, WA 98111
"Business-(CEO) Airborne"

John R. Cochran
III Cascade Plaza
Akron, OH 44308
"Business-(CEO) FirstMerit"

Ross Cockrell
701 N. Brazos St., Suite 1400
Austin, Texas 78701
"Business-Venture Capitalist"

Vance D. Coffman
6801 Rockledge Drive
Bethesda, MD 20817
"Business-(CEO) Lockheed Martin"

Gill Cogan
2882 Sand Hill Road, Suite 106
Menlo Park, CA 94025
"Business-Venture Capitalist"

Millionaire Directory 2nd edition

Alan Cohen
4955 Orange Drive
Davie, FL 33314
"Business-(CEO) Andrx Group"

William T. Coleman III
2315 North First Street
San Jose, CA 95131
"Business-(CEO) BEA Systems"

Bud Colligan
428 University Avenue
Palo Alto, CA 94301
"Business-Venture Capitalist"

Arthur Collins, Jr
7000 Central Avenue NE
Minneapolis, MN 55432-
"Business-(CEO) Medtronic"

Duane E. Collins
6035 Parkland Blvd.
Cleveland, OH 44124
"Business- (CEO) Parker-Hannifin"

J. Edmund Colloton
1400 Old Country Road, Suite 109
Westbury, NY 11590
"Business-Venture Capitalist"

Gary Campbell Comer
2 Lands' End Lane
Dodgeville, WI 53595
"Business-Lands' End Founder"

Douglas Conant
Campbell Place
Camden, NJ 08103
"Business-(CEO) Campbell Soup"

Charles Conaway
3100 West Big Beaver Road
Troy, MI 48084
"Business-(CEO) Kmart"

Philip Condit
P.O. Box 3707
Seattle, WA 98124
"Business-(CEO) Boeing"

Robert J. Congel
4 Clinton Square
Syracuse, NY 13212
"Business-Shopping Malls"

Grover Connell
45 Cardinal Drive
Westfield, NJ 07090
"Business-Equipment Leasing"

Christopher M. Connor
101 Prospect Avenue NW
Cleveland, OH 44115
"Business-(CEO) Sherwin-Williams"

Craig A. Conway
4460 Hacienda Drive
Pleasanton, CA 94588
"Business-(CEO) PeopleSoft"

John Conway
One Crown Way
Philadelphia, PA 19154
"Business-(CEO) Crown Cork & Seal"

Scott D. Cook
2535 Garcia Avenue
Mountainview, CA 94043
"Business-Intuit Founder"

William Alfred Cook
P.O. Box 489
Bloomington, IN 47402
"Business-Medical Devices"

William A. Cooper
801 Marquette Avenue
Minneapolis, MN 55402-3475
"Business-(CEO) TCF Financial"

Millionaire Directory 2nd edition

William K. Coors
17735 West 32nd Avenue
Golden, CO 80401
"Business-Beer"

Eric Copeland
2494 Sand Hill Road, Suite 200
Menlo Park, CA 94025
"Business-Venture Capitalist"

Helen Kinney Copley
7776 Ivanhoe Avenue
LaJolla, CA 92037
"Business-Publishing"

Luke R. Corbett
P.O. Box 25861
Oklahoma City, OK 73125
"Business-(CEO) Kerr-McGee"

Alston D. Correll
P.O. Box 105605
Atlanta, GA 30348
"Business-(CEO) Georgia-Pacific"

Wilfred Corrigan
1551 McCarty Blvd.
Milpitas, CA 95035
"Business-(CEO) LSI Logic"

Charles Cory
c/o Morgan Stanley
1585 Broadway
New York, NY 10036
"Business-Banker"

Howard E. Cosgrove
P.O. Box 231
Wilmington, DE 19899
"Business-(CEO) Conectiv"

David Cote
1900 Richmond Road
Cleveland, OH 44124
"Business-(CEO) TRW"

Charles H. Cotros
1390 Enclave Parkway
Houston, TX 77077
"Business-(CEO) Sysco"

Christos Cotsakos
4500 Bohannon Drive
Menlo Park, CA 94025
"Business-(CEO) E*Trade"

Gary L. Countryman
600 Atlantic Avenue
Boston, MA 02210
"Business-(CEO) Liberty Financial Companiess"

Arthur W. Coviello, Jr
20 Crosby Drive
Bedford, MA 01730
"Business-(CEO) RSA Security"

David Cowan
535 Middlefield Road, Suite 245
Menlo Park, CA 94025
"Business-Venture Capitalist"

Ann Cox-Chambers
1400 Lake Hearn Drive NE
Atlanta, GA 30319
"Business-Media"

Barbara Cox-Anthony
1400 Lake Hearn Drive NE
Atlanta, GA 30319
"Business-Media"

Howard Cox
880 Winter Street
Waltham, MA 02451
"Business-Venture Capitalist"

Tench Coxe
755 Page Mill Road, Suite #A-200
Palo Alto, CA 94304
"Business-Venture Capitalist"

Millionaire Directory 2nd edition

Edwin M. Crawford
3000 Galleria Tower
Birmingham, AL 35244
"Business-(CEO) Caremark Rx"

John W. Creighton
P.O. Box 66100
Chicago, IL 60666
"Business-(CEO) UAL"

Michael J. Critelli
1 Elmcroft Road
Stamford, CT 06926
"Business-(CEO) Pitney Bowes"

James Q. Crowe
1025 Eldorado Boulevard
Broomfield, CO 68131
"Business-(CEO) Level 3 Communications"

Lester Crown
222 North LaSalle Street
Chicago, IL 60601
"Business-General Dynamics"

Mark Cuban
777 Sport Street
Dallas, TX 75207
"Entertainment-Sports Team Owner"

H. Lawrence Culp, Jr
1250 24th Street NW
Washington, DC 20037
"Business-(CEO) Danahe"

Curt Culver
P.O. Box 488
Milwaukee, WI 53201
"Business-(CEO) MCIC Investment"

Paul J. Curlander
740 West New Circle Road
Lexington, KY 40550
"Business-(CEO) Lexmark International"

Raymond M. Curran
150 North Michigan Avenue
Chicago, IL 60601
"Business-(CEO) Smurfit-Stone"

Peter L.S. Currie
c/o General Atlantic Partners
Three Pickwick Plaza
Greenwich, CT 06830
"Business-Venture Capitalist"

Alexander Cutler
1111 Superior Avenue
Cleveland, OH 44114
"Business-(CEO) Eaton"

John Daane
101 Innovation Drive
San Jose, CA 95134
"Business-(CEO) Altera"

David A. Daberko
1900 East Ninth Street
Cleveland, OH 44114
"Business-(CEO) National City"

Douglas Daft
P.O. Box 1734
Atlanta, GA 30301
Business-(CEO) Coca-Cola"

Yogen Dalal
2800 Sand Hill Road, Suite 250
Menlo Park, CA 94025
"Business-Venture Capitalist"

Richard Dale
20 Custom House Street, Suite 830
Boston, MA 02110
"Business-Venture Capitalist"

Millionaire Directory　　　　　　　　　　　　2nd edition

David D'Allesandro
P.O. Box 111
Boston, MA 02117
"Business-(CEO) John Hancock Financial"

Michael T. Dan
P.O. Box 18100
Richmond, VA 23226
"Business-(CEO) Pittston"

Thomas Dattilo
P.O. Box 550
Findlay, OH 45839
"Business-(CEO) Cooper Tire & Rubber"

Richard E. Dauch
1840 Holbrook Avenue
Detroit, MI 48212
"Business-(CEO) American Axle"

George David
One Financial Plaza
Hartford, CT 06101
"Business-CEO (United Technologies)"

Williams Davidow
2775 Sand Hill Road, Suite 240
Menlo Park, CA 94025
"Business-Venture Capitalist"

Charles Davidson
350 Glenborough
Houston, TX 77067
"Business-(CEO) Noble Affiliates"

Richard K. Davidson
1416 Dodge Street
Omaha, NE 68179
"Business-(CEO) Union Pacific"

William Morse Davidson
2300 Harmon Road
Auburn Hills, MI 48326
"Business-Guardian Industries"

Thomas E. Davin
11150 Santa Monica Blvd. Suite 1200
Los Angeles, CA 90025
"Business-Venture Capitalist"

Don H. Davis, Jr
777 East Wisconsin Avenue
Milwaukee, WI 53202
"Business-(CEO) Rockwell International"

Erroll B. Davis, Jr
P.O. Box 2568
Madison, WI 53701
"Business-(CEO) Alliant Energy"

Marvin Davis
2121 Avenue of the Stars #2800
Los Angeles, CA 90067
"Business-Real Estate"

William E. Davis
300 Erie Blvd. West
Syracuse, NY 13202
"Business-(CEO) Niagara Mohawk"

William L. Davis
77 West Wacker Drive
Chicago, IL 60601
"Business-(CEO) R.R. Donnelley"

Robert Davoli
20 Custom House Street, Suite 830
Boston, MA 02110
"Business-Venture Capitalist"

James Day
13135 South Dairy Ashford
Sugar Land, TX 77478
"Business-(CEO) Noble Drilling"

Howard M. Dean
3600 North River Road
Franklin Park, IL 60131
"Business-(CEO) Dean Foods"

Millionaire Directory

2nd edition

Ken DeAngelis
701 N. Brazos St., Suite 1400
Austin, Texas 78701
"Business-Venture Capitalist"

Earnest W. Deavenport, Jr
P.O. Box 511
Kingsport, TN 37662
"Business-(CEO) Eastman Chemical"

Edward John Debartolo, Jr.
P.O. Box 9128
Youngtown, OH 44513
"Business-Shopping Center"

Robert Henry Dedman Sr.
3030 LBJ Freeway #700
Dallas, TX 75234
"Business-Country Clubs"

Christel Dehaan
10 Market Street #1990
Indianapolis, IN 46204
"Business-Time Shares"

Michael Dell
One Dell Way
Round Rock, TX 78682
"Business-Dell Computer Founder"

Harris DeLoach, Jr
P.O. Box 160
Hartsville, SC 29551
"Business-(CEO) Sonoco Products"

Claiborne Deming
P.O. Box 7000
El Dorado, AR 71731
"Business-(CEO) Murphy Oil"

Paul Deninger
950 Tower Lane, 18th Floor
Foster City, CA 94404
"Business-Venture Capitalist"

Steven A. Denning
c/o General Atlantic Partners
Three Pickwick Plaza
Greenwich, CT 06830
"Business-Venture Capitalist"

John M. Derrick, Jr
1900 Pennsylvania Avenue NW
Washington, DC 20068
"Business-(CEO) Potomac Electric"

Michael Devlin
18880 Homestead Road
Cupertino, CA 95014
"Business-(CEO) Rational Software"

Robert M. Devlin
P.O. Box 3247
Houston, TX 77253
"Business- (CEO) American General"

Richard M. DeVos
7575 Fulton Street
Ada, MI 49355
"Business-Amway Co-Founder"

John C. Dicus
700 South Kansas Avenue
Topeka, KS 66603
"Business-(CEO) Capitol Federal Financial"

William Dillard II
1600 Cantrell Road
Little Rock, AR 72201
"Business-(CEO) Dillard's"

Barry Diller
152 West 57th Street, 42nd Floor
New York, NY 10009
"Entertainment-Television"

John T. Dillon
Two Manhattanville Road
Purchase, NY 10577
"Business- (CEO) International Paper"

Millionaire Directory   2nd edition

Daniel DiMicco
2100 Rexford Road
Charlotte, NC 28211
"Business-(CEO) Nucor"

James Dimon
One Bank One Plaza
Chicago, IL 60670
"Business-(CEO) Bank One"

John Dirvin
701 N. Brazos St., Suite 1400
Austin, Texas 78701
"Business-Venture Capitalist"

Roy Disney
500 South Buena Vista Street
Burbank, CA 91521
"Entertainment-Disney Stocks"

Steven Dodge
116 Huntington Avenue
Boston, MA 02116
"Business-CEO (American Tower)"

Walter A. Dods, Jr
P.O. Box 3200
Honolulu, HI 96847
"Business-(CEO) BancWest"

John L. Doerr
2750 Sand Hill Road
Menlo Park, CA 94025
"Business-Venture Capital"

Harold Doherty
15 Beach Street
Staten Island, NY 10304
"Business-(CEO) Staten Island Bancorp"

Charles Francis Dolan
1111 Stewart Avenue
Bethpage, NY 11714
"Business-Cabel TV"

James L. Dolan
1111 Stewart Avenue
Bethpage, NY 11714
"Business- (CEO) Cablevision Systems"

Peter Dolan
345 Park Avenue
New York, NY 10154
"Business-(CEO) Bristol-Myers Squibb"

Ronald W. Dollens
P.O. Box 44906
Indianapolis, IN 46244
"Business-(CEO) Guidant"

Timothy Donahue
2001 Edmund Halley Drive
Reston, VA 20191
"Business-(CEO) Nextel Communications"

John Dooner, Jr
1271 Avenue of the Americas
New York, NY 10020
"Business-(CEO) Interpublic Group"

Bennett Dorrance
Campbell Place
Camden, NJ 08103
"Business-Campbell Soup"

Jim Dorrian
The Pioneer Hotel Building
2925 Woodside Road
Woodside, CA 94062
"Business-Venture Capitalist"

Steven J. Douglass
3231 East 6th Street
Topeka, KS 66607
"Business-(CEO) Payless ShoeSource"

Rodger B. Dowdell, Jr
132 Fairgrounds Road
West Kingston, RI 02892
"Business-(CEO) America Power Conversion"

Millionaire Directory

2nd edition

E. Linn Draper, Jr
1 Riverside Plaza
Columbus, OH 43215
"Business-(CEO) American Electric"

Timothy C. Draper
DFJ, 400 Seaport Court, Suite 250
Redwood City, CA 94063
"Business-Venture Capitalist"

Jeffrey M. Drazan
3000 Sand Hill Road,
Building 4, Suite 240
Menlo Park, CA 94025
"Business-Venture Capitalist"

Millard Drexler
One Harrison Street
San Francisco, CA 94105
"Business-(CEO) Gap"

John Drosdick
1801 Market Street
Philadelphia, PA 19103
"Business-(CEO) Sunoco"

Stanley Druckenmiller
900 Third Avenue, 29th Floor
New York, NY 10022
"Business-Investments"

David A. Duffield
4460 Hacienda Drive
Pleasanton, CA 94588
"Business-PeopleSoft"

Archie W. Dunham
600 North Dairy Ashford
Houston, TX 77079
"Business-(CEO) Conoco"

Duane R. Dunham
1170 Eighth Avenue
Bethlehem, PA 18016
"Business-(CEO) Bethlehem Steel"

Bruce Dunlevie
2480 Sand Hill Rd., Suite 200
Menlo Park, CA 94025
"Business-Venture Capitalist"

Henry Duques
5660 New Northside Drive
Atlanta, GA 30328
"Business-(CEO) First Data"

Bernard J. Duroc-Danner
515 Oak Post Boulevard
Houston, TX 77027
"Business-(CEO) Weatherford International"

Tom Dyal
3000 Sand Hill Rd., Bldg. 2, Suite 290
Menlo Park, CA 94025
"Business-Venture Capitalist"

Mark F. Dziaglga
c/o General Atlantic Partners
Three Pickwick Plaza
Greenwich, CT 06830
"Business-Venture Capitalist"

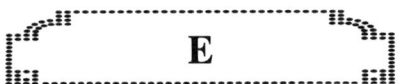

Anthony F. Earley, Jr
2000 Second Avenue
Detroit, MI 48226
"Business-(CEO) DTE Energy"

Bernard Ebbers
500 Clinton Center Drive
Clinton, MS 39056
"Business-(CEO) Worldcom"

Millionaire Directory 2nd edition

Robert Eckert
333 Continental Blvd.
El Segundo, CA 90245
"Business- (CEO) Mattel"

John Edwardson
200 North Milwaukee Ave
Vernon Hills, IL 60061
"Business-(CEO) CDW Computer Centers"

Janet Effland
Apax, 445 Park Ave.
New York, NY 10022
"Business-Venture Capitalist"

Michael Egan
200 South Andrews Avenue
Fort Lauderdale, FL 33301
"Business-(CEO) ANC Rental"

Richard J. Egan
Embassy of the U. S. A.
42 Elgin Road
Dublin 4, Ireland
""Business- Software (EMC)"

Barry Eggers
2882 Sand Hill Road, Suite 106
Menlo Park, CA 94025
"Business-Venture Capitalist"

Warren Eisenberg
650 Liberty Avenue
Union, NJ 07083
"Business-(CEO) Bed Bath & Beyond"

Michael D. Eisner
500 South Buena Vista Street
Burbank, CA 91521
"Business-(CEO) Disney"

Richard G. Ellenberger
P.O. Box 2301
Cincinnati, OH 45201
"Business-(CEO) Broadwing"

Alec Ellison
950 Tower Lane, 18th Floor
Foster City, CA 94404
"Business-Venture Capitalist"

Lawrence Joseph Ellison
500 Oracle Parkway
Redwood City, CA 94065
"Business-(CEO) Oracle"

Bill Elmore
70 Willow Rd, Suite 200
Menlo Park, CA 94025
"Business-Venture Capitalist"

Gary Ely
P.O. Box 3727
Spokane, WA 99220
"Business-(CEO) Avista"

Archie "Red" Emmerson
19794 Riverside Ave.
Anderson, CA 96007
"Business-Timber"

George L. Engelke, Jr
One Astoria Federal Plaza
Lake Success, NY 11042-
"Business-(CEO) Astoria Financial"

Thomas Engibous
P.O. Box 660199
Dallas, TX 75266
"Business-(CEO) Texas Instruments"

Gregg Engles
2515 McKinney Avenue
Dallas, TX 75201
"Business-(CEO) Suiza Foods"

Edmond J. English
770 Cochituate Road
Framingham, MA 01701
"Business-(CEO) TJX Companies"

Millionaire Directory 2nd edition

Erik Engstrom
c/o General Atlantic Partners
Three Pickwick Plaza
Greenwich, CT 06830
"Business-Venture Capitalist"

Roger A. Enrico
700 Anderson Hill Road
Purchase, NY 10577
"Business-(CEO) Pepsico"

Charles Ergen
5701 South Santa Fe Drive
Littleton, CO 80120
"Business-(CEO) EchoStar Communications"

Bill Ericson
505 Fifth Avenue South, Suite 610
Seattle, WA 98104
"Business-Venture Capitalist"

Mark Ernst
4400 Main Street
Kansas City, MO 64111
"Business-(CEO) H&R Block"

William T. Esrey
P.O. Box 11315
Kansas City, MO 64112
"Business-(CEO) Sprint FON"

Robert Essner
Five Giralda Farms
Madison, NJ 07940
"Business-(CEO) American Home Products"

Judith Estrin
2465 Latham Street, 3rd Floor
Mountain View, CA 94040
"Business-(CEO) Packet Design"

Joseph R. Ettore
2418 Main Street
Rocky Hill, CT 06067
"Business-(CEO) Ames Dept. Stores"

Richard W. Evans, Jr
P.O. Box 1600
San Antonio, TX 78296
"Business-(CEO) Cullen/Frost Bankers"

Roger Evans
2929 Campus Dr., Suite 400
San Mateo, CA 94403
"Business-Venture Capitalist"

Tony Evnin
30 Rockefeller Plaza, Room 5508
New York, NY 10112
"Business-Venture Capitalist"

John Eyler, Jr
461 From Road
Paramus, NJ 07652
"Business-(CEO) Toys `R' Us"

Robert A. Fabbio
12416 Hymeadow Drive, Suite 200
Austin, Texas 78750
"Business-(CEO) VIEO"

Robert D. Fagan
P.O. Box 111
Tampa, FL 33601
"Business-(CEO) TECO Energy"

Richard Fairbank
2980 Fairview Park Drive
Falls Church, VA 22042
"Business-(CEO) Capital One Financial"

Richard T. Farmer
P.O. Box 625737
Cincinnati, OH 45262
"Business-Cintas"

Millionaire Directory   2nd edition

David Farr
P.O.. Box 4100
St Louis, MO 63136
"Business-(CEO) Emerson Electric"

W. James Farrell
3600 West Lake Avenue
Glenview, IL 60025
"Business-(CEO) Illionis Tool Works"

Irwin Federman
2180 San Hill Road, Suite #300
Menlo Park, CA 94025
"Business-Venture Capitalist"

Jonathan Feiber
2775 Sand Hill Road, Suite 240
Menlo Park, CA 94025
"Business-Venture Capitalist"

Kenneth Feld
8607 Westwood Center Drive
Vienna, VA 22182
"Entertainment-Circus Owner"

E. James Ferland
80 Park Plaza
Newark, NJ 07102
"Business-(CEO) Pub. Svc. Enterprise"

Paul J. Ferri
Bay Colony Corporate Center
1000 Winter St., Suite 4500
Waltham, MA 02451
"Business-Venture Capitalist"

Michael Feuer
P.O. Box 228070
Shaker Heights, OH 44122
"Business-(CEO) OfficeMax"

Joseph Ficalora
615 Merrick Avenue
Westbury, NY 11590
"Business-(CEO) New York Community"

Fredrick Woodruff (Ted) Field
10900 Wilshire Blvd. #1400
Los Angeles, CA 90024
"Business-Media"

Frank Filipps
1601 Market Street
Philadelphia, PA 19103
"Business-(CEO) Radian Group"

David Filo
3420 Central Expy. #201
Santa Clara, CA 95051
"Business-Yahoo!"

Lawrence G. Finch
1600 El Camino Real, Suite 280
Menlo Park, CA 94025
"Business-Venture Capitalist"

Carleton Fiorina
3000 Hanover Street
Palo Alto, CA 94304
"Business-(CEO) Hewlett-Packard"

Donald George Fisher
One Harrison Street
San Francisco, CA 94105
"Business-Gap"

Doris Feigenbaum Fisher
One Harrison Street
San Francisco, CA 94105
"Business-Gap"

John H. N. Fisher
DFJ, 400 Seaport Court, Suite 250
Redwood City, CA 94063
"Business-Venture Capitalist"

John J. Fisher
One Harrison Street
San Francisco, CA 94105
"Business-Gap"

Millionaire Directory   2nd edition

Robert J. Fisher
One Harrison Street
San Francisco, CA 94105
"Business-Gap"

Alan Fishman
195 Montague Street
Brooklyn, NY 11201
"Business-(CEO) Independence Community"

Jerald Fishman
One Technology Way
Norwood, MA 02062
"Business-CEO (Analog Devices)"

William A. Fitzgerald
2120 South 72nd Street
Omaha, NE 68124
"Business-(CEO) Commercial Federal"

Barry J. Fitzpatrick
6400 Arlington Boulevard
Falls Church, VA 22042
"Business-(CEO) First Virginia Banks"

Jim Flach
428 University Avenue
Palo Alto, CA 94301
"Business-Venture Capitalist"

Kevin Fong
2800 Sand Hill Road, Suite 250
Menlo Park, CA 94025
"Business-Venture Capitalist"

Jennifer Scott Fonstad
DFJ, 400 Seaport Court, Suite 250
Redwood City, CA 94063
"Business-Venture Capitalist"

William C. Foote
P.O. Box 6721
Chicago, IL 60680
"Business-(CEO) USG"

Gerald J. Ford
135 Main Street
San Francisco, CA 94105
"Business-(CEO) Golden State Bancorp"

William Clay Ford
P.O. Box 6012
Dearborn, MI 48342
"Business-Ford Motor Co."

Joe T. Ford
One Allied Drive
Little Rock, AR 72202
"Business-(CEO) Alltel"

William Ford
P.O. Box 1899
Dearborn, MI 48121
"Business-(CEO) Ford Motor Company"

William E. Ford
c/o General Atlantic Partners
Three Pickwick Plaza
Greenwich, CT 06830
"Business-Venture Capitalist"

James J. Forese
70 Valley Stream Parkway
Malvern, PA 19355
"Business-(CEO) IKON Office Solutions"

Theodore Forstmann
767 Fifth Avenue
New York, NY 10153
"Business-Leveraged Buyouts"

Kent B. Foster
1600 East St Andrew Place
Santa Ana, CA 92705
"Business-(CEO) Ingram Micro"

James C. France
1801 West International Speedway Blvd.
Daytona Beach, FL 32114
"Entertainment-NASCAR"

Millionaire Directory   2nd edition

William C. France, Jr.
1801 West International Speedway Blvd.
Daytona Beach, FL 32114
"Entertainment-NASCAR"

H. Allen Franklin
270 Peachtree Street
Atlanta, GA 30303
"Business-(CEO) Southern Co."

Tom Frederick
2494 Sand Hill Road, Suite 200
Menlo Park, CA 94025
"Business-Venture Capitalist"

Kenneth Freeman
One Malcolm Avenue
Teterboro, NJ 07608
"Business-(CEO) Quest Diagnostics"

David French
4210 South Industrial Drive
Austin, TX 78744
"Business-(CEO) Cirrus Logic"

Thomas Friedkin
1101 Wilshire Place Drive
Houston, TX 77040
"Business-Gulf State Toyota"

Mark P. Frissora
500 North Field Drive
Lake Forest, IL 60045
"Business-(CEO) Tenneco Automotive"

Thomas F. Frist, Jr.
P.O. Box 550
Nashville, TN 37202
"Business-Healthcare"

Edward Fritzky
51 University Street
Seattle, WA 98101
"Business-(CEO) Immunex"

Phillip Frost
4400 Biscayne Boulevard
Miami, FL 33137-3227
"Business-(CEO) IVAX"

Richard S. Fuld, Jr.
3 World Financial Center
New York, NY 10285
"Business-(CEO) Lehman Bros."

S. Marce Fuller
1155 Perimeter Center West
Atlanta, GA 30338
"Business-(CEO) Mirant"

Rufus A. Fulton, Jr
P.O. Box 4887
Lancaster, PA 17604
"Business-(CEO) Fulton Financial"

Christopher Gabrieli
83 Walnut Street
Wellesley Hills, MA 02481
"Business-Venture Capitalist"

Barbara Carlson Gage
P.O. Box 59159
Minneapolis, MN 55459
"Business-Travel Services"

James C. Gaither
755 Page Mill Road, Suite #A-200
Palo Alto, CA 94304
"Business-Venture Capitalist"

Jerry Gallagher
1 Gorham Island
Westport, CT 06880
"Business-Venture Capitalist"

Millionaire Directory   2nd edition

Robert C. Gallagher
1200 Hansen Road
Green Bay, WI 54304
"Business-(CEO) Associated Banc-Corp"

Thomas Gallagher
3930 Howard Hughes Parkway
Las Vegas, NV 89109
"Business-(CEO) Park Place Entertainment"

Joseph Galli, Jr.
29 East Stephenson Street
Freeport, IL 61032
"Business-(CEO) Newell Rubbermaid"

Ernest Gallo
P.O. Box 1130
Meodesto, CA 95354
"Business-Wine (Gallo)"

Christopher B. Galvin
1303 East Algonquin Road
Schaumburg, IL 60196
"Business-(CEO) Motorola"

Albert R. Gamper, Jr
1211 Avenue of the Americas
New York, NY 10036
"Business-(CEO) CIT Group"

Sameer Gandhi
3000 Sand Hill Road
Bldg. 4, Suite 180
Menlo Park, CA 94025
"Business-Venture Capitalist"

Rakesh Gangwal
2345 Crystal Drive
Arlington, VA 22227
"Business-CEO (US Airways Group)"

Robert P. Gannon
40 East Broadway
Butte, MT 59701
"Business-(CEO) Montana Power"

C. Stedman Garber, Jr
2 Lincoln Centre
Dallas, TX 75240
"Business-(CEO) Santa Fe International"

Gaurav Garg
3000 Sand Hill Road
Bldg. 4, Suite 180
Menlo Park, CA 94025
"Business-Venture Capitalist"

Terence J. Garnett
2494 Sand Hill Road, Suite 200
Menlo Park, CA 94025
"Business-Venture Capitalist"

Stephen A. Garofalo
One North Lexington Avenue
White Plains, NY 10601
"Business-(CEO) Metromedia Fiber Net"

Jeff Garvey
701 N. Brazos St., Suite 1400
Austin, Texas 78701
"Business-Venture Capitalist"

Charles Cassius Gates, Jr.
3773 Cherry Creek North Drive #680
Denver, CO 80209
"Business-Gates Corp."

William "Bill" Gates III
One Microsoft Way
Redmond, WA 98052
"Business- Software (Microsoft)"

Jean Gaulin
P.O. Box 696000
San Antonio, TX 78269
"Business-(CEO) Ultramar Diamond"

Edward Lewis Gaylord
1506 Dorchester Drive
Oklahoma City, OK 73114
"Business-Media"

Millionaire Directory   2nd edition

David Geffen
100 Universal City Plaza, Bldg. 477
Universal City, CA 91608
"Business-Entertainment"

Jay M. Gellert
21650 Oxnard Street
Woodland Hills, CA 91367
"Business-(CEO) Health Net"

S. Craig George
110 West Seventh Street
Tulsa, OK 74119
"Business-(CEO) Vintage Petroleum"

Alan Gerry
One Cablevision Center
P.O. Box 311
Liberty, NY 12754
"Business-Cable Television"

Lousi Gerstner, Jr.
c/o I.B.M.
New Orchard Road
Armonk, NY 10504
"Business-I.B.M."

Gordon Peter Getty
2880 Broadway
San Francisco, CA 94115
"Business-Inheritance (Oil)"

Samir G. Gibara
1144 East Market Street
Akron, OH 44316
"Business-(CEO) Goodyear"

Vincent A. Gierer, Jr
100 West Putnam Avenue
Greenwich, CT 06830
"Business-(CEO) UST, Inc."

John F. Gifford
120 San Gabriel Drive
Sunnyvale, CA 94086
"Business-(CEO) Maxim intergrated Pro."

Kevin B. Gifford
11150 Santa Monica Blvd. Suite 1200
Los Angeles, CA 90025
"Business-Venture Capitalist"

Raymond V. Gilmartin
P.O. Box 100
Whitehouse Station, NJ 08889
"Business-(CEO) Merck"

Louis Giuliano
4 West Red Oak Lane
White Plains, NY 10604
"Business-(CEO) ITT Industries"

Alfred R. Glancy III
500 Griswold Street
Detroit, MI 48226
"Business-(CEO) MCN Energy Group"

Ed Glassmeyer
1 Gorham Island
Westport, CT 06880
"Business-Venture Capitalist"

Guilford Glazer
9440 Santa Monica Blvd. #610
Beverly Hills, CA 90210
"Business-Real Estate"

Malcolm Glazer
One Buccaneer Place
Tampa, FL 33607
"Business-Investments, Sports Team"

Robert D. Glynn, Jr
One Market, Spear Tower
San Francisco, CA 94105
"Business-(CEO) PG&E"

Jim Goetz
428 University Avenue
Palo Alto, CA 94301
"Business-Venture Capitalist"

Millionaire Directory   2nd edition

Michael Goguen
3000 Sand Hill Road
Bldg. 4, Suite 180
Menlo Park, CA 94025
"Business-Venture Capitalist"

David Gold
4000 Union Pacific Avenue
City of Commerce, CA 90023
"Business- (CEO) 99¢ only stores"

Bruce Golden
428 University Avenue
Palo Alto, CA 94301
"Business-Venture Capitalist"

Richard N. Goldman
One Lombard Street #303
San Francisco, CA 94111
"Business-Levi Strauss"

Russell Goldsmith
400 North Roxbury Drive
Beverly Hills, CA 90210
"Business-(CEO) City National"

Robert Goldstein
1840 Gateway Drive
San Mateo, CA 94404
"Business-(CEO) Bay View Capital"

Blase Thomas Golisano
911 Panorama Trail South
Rochester, NY 14625
"Business-(CEO) Paychex"

Louis Gonda
1999 Avenue of the Stars, 39th Fl.
Los Angeles, CA 90067
"Business-(Executive) ILFC"

David R. Goode
Three Commercial Place
Norfolk, VA 235101
"Business-(CEO) Norfolk Southern"

Robert P. Goodman
1865 Palmer Avenue, Suite 104
Larchmont, NY 10538
"Business-Venture Capitalist"

James Goodnight
100 Sas Campus Drive
Cary, NC 27513
"Business-Software"

Paul Goodrich
1000 Second Ave., Ste. 3700
Seattle, WA 98104
"Business-Venture Capitalist"

Tom T. Gores
2949 Century Park East #2700
Los Angeles, CA 90067
"Business-Leveraged Buyouts"

Thomas Gossage
Hercules Plaza
Wilmington, DE 19894
"Business-(CEO) Hercules"

Bill Gossman
2775 Sand Hill Road, Suite 240
Menlo Park, CA 94025
"Business-Venture Capitalist"

Greg Gottesman
1000 Second Ave., Ste. 3700
Seattle, WA 98104
"Business-Venture Capitalist"

Kathryn Gould
70 Willow Rd, Suite 200
Menlo Park, CA 94025
"Business-Venture Capitalist"

William O. Grabe
c/o General Atlantic Partners
Three Pickwick Plaza
Greenwich, CT 06830
"Business-Venture Capitalist"

Millionaire Directory   2nd edition

Donald E. Graham
1150 15th Street NW
Washington, DC 20071
"Business-(CEO) Washington Post"

William Greehey
P.O. Box 500
San Antonio, TX 78292
"Business-(CEO) Valero Energy"

Joshus Green III
1932 Blenheim Drive East
Seattle, WA 98112
"Business-Inheritance (PeopleBank)"

Richard C. Green, Jr
P.O. Box 13287
Kansas City, MO 64199
"Business-(CEO) UtiliCorp United"

Jack M. Greenberg
One Kroc Drive
Oak Brook, IL 60523
"Business-(CEO) McDonald"

Jeffrey W. Greenberg
1166 Avenue of the Americas
New York, NY 10036
Business-(CEO) Marsh & McLennan"

Maurice "Hank" Greenberg
70 Pine Street
New York, NY 10270
"Business-(CEO) A.I.G."

John M. Gregory
501 - 5th Street
Bristol, TN 37620
"Business-(CEO) King Pharmaceuticals"

Gregory C. Gretsch
1600 El Camino Real, Suite 280
Menlo Park, CA 94025
"Business-Venture Capitalist"

William "Bill" Gross
130 W. Union Street
Pasadena, CA 91103
"Business-(CEO) Idealab"

Adam Grosser
70 Willow Rd, Suite 200
Menlo Park, CA 94025
"Business-Venture Capitalist"

Dan Grossman
30 Rockefeller Plaza, Room 5508
New York, NY 10112
"Business-Venture Capitalist"

Andy Grove
2200 Mission College Blvd.
Santa Clara, CA 95052
"Business-(CEO) Intel"

Robert Grubbs
4711 Golf Road
Skokie, IL 60076
"Business-(CEO) Anixter International"

Jerry A. Grundhofer
601 Second Avenue South
Minneapolis, MN 55402
"Business-(CEO) US Bancorp."

Leonard S. Gudelski
West 80 Century Road
Paramus, NJ 07652
"Business-(CEO) Hudson City Bancorp"

Paul Gudonis
3 Van de Graaff Drive
Burlington, MA 01803
"Business-(CEO) Genuity"

Tim Guleri
3000 Sand Hill Road,
Building 4, Suite 240
Menlo Park, CA 94025
"Business-Venture Capitalist"

Millionaire Directory   2nd edition

Robert Gunderson, Jr.
155 Constitution Drive
Menlo Park, CA 94025
"Professional-Lawyer"

Rajiv L. Gupta
100 Independence Mall West
Philadelphia, PA 19106
"Business-(CEO) Rohm and Haas"

Bill Gurley
2480 Sand Hill Rd., Suite 200
Menlo Park, CA 94025
"Business-Venture Capitalist"

Carlos M. Gutierrez
One Kellogg Square
Battle Creek, MI 49016
"Business-(CEO) Kellogg"

Clifford l. Haas
1600 El Camino Real, Suite 280
Menlo Park, CA 94025
"Business-Venture Capitalist"

James Hackett
1001 Fannin Street
Houston, TX 77002-
"Business-(CEO) Ocean Energy"

James P. Hackett
901 - 44th Street
Grand Rapids, MI 49508
"Business-(CEO) Steelcase"

Leonard A. Hadley
403 West Fourth Street North
Newton, IA 50208
"Business-(CEO) Maytag"

Fred D. Hafer
P.O. Box 1957
Morristown, NJ 07962
"Business-(CEO) GPU"

Pamela Hagenah
2750 Sand Hill Rd.
Menlo Park, CA 94025
"Business-Venture Capitalist"

David Halbert
5215 North O'Connor Blvd.
Irving, TX 75039
"Business-(CEO) AdvancePCS"

Roy W. Haley
Commerce Court
Pittsburgh, PA 15219
"Business-(CEO) Wesco International"

Tim Haley
3000 Sand Hill Rd., Bldg. 2, Suite 290
Menlo Park, CA 94025
"Business-Venture Capitalist"

Kevin G. Hall
525 University Avenue, Suite 800
Palo Alto, CA 94301
"Business-Venture Capitalist"

Brian Halla
P.O. Box 58090
Santa Clara, CA 95052
"Business-(CEO) National Semiconductor"

William Hallinan
4800 North Scottsdale Road
Scottsdale, AZ 85251
"Business-(CEO) Finova Group"

Cinda Hallman
2050 Spectrum Blvd.
Fort Lauderdale, FL 33309
"Business-(CEO) Spherion"

Millionaire Directory   2nd edition

John H. Hammergren
One Post Street
San Francisco, CA 94104
"Business-(CEO) McKesson HBOC"

Thomas Hammond
2600 Telegraph Road
Bloomfield Hills, MI 48302
"Business-(CEO) Flagstar Bancorp"

Ellen M. Hancock
2831 Mission College Blvd.
Santa Clara, CA 95054
"Business-(CEO) Exodus Communications"

William J. Hannigan
4255 Amon Carter Blvd.
Fort Worth, TX 76155
"Business-(CEO) Sabre Holding"

Mark S. Hansen
1945 Lakepointe Drive
Lewisville, TX 75057
"Business-(CEO) Fleming Companies"

H. Edward Hanway
One Liberty Place
Philadelphia, PA 19192
"Business-(CEO) Cigna"

Promod Haque
525 University Avenue, Suite 800
Palo Alto, CA 94301
"Business-Venture Capitalist"

George J. Harad
P.O. Box 50
Boise, ID 83728
"Business-(CEO) Boise Cascade"

Eli Harari
140 Caspian Court
Sunnyvale, CA 94089
"Business-(CEO) SanDisk"

Raymond Harbert
One Riverchase Parkway South
Birmingham, AL 35244
"Business-Money Manager"

G. Felda Hardymon
83 Walnut Street
Wellesley Hills, MA 02481
"Business-Venture Capitalist"

Fred Harman
525 University Avenue, Suite 1300
Palo Alto, CA 94301
"Business-Venture Capitalist"

Henry H. Harrell
P.O. Box 25099
Richmond, VA 23260
"Business-(CEO) Universal"

William B. Harrison Jr
270 Park Avenue
New York, NY 10017
"Business-(CEO) J.P. Morgan"

David R. Harvey
3050 Spruce Street
St Louis, MO 63103
"Business-(CEO) Sigma-Aldrich"

Kevin Harvey
2480 Sand Hill Rd., Suite 200
Menlo Park, CA 94025
"Business-Venture Capitalist"

William Haseltine
9410 Key West Avenue
Rockville, MD 20850
"Business-(CEO) Human Genome Sciences"

Fred Hassan
100 Route 206 North
Peapack, NJ 07977
"Business-(CEO) Pharmacia"

Millionaire Directory   2nd edition

Alan G. Hassenfeld
1011 Newport Avenue
Pawtucket, RI 02862
"Business-(CEO) Hasbro"

Dave Hathaway
30 Rockefeller Plaza, Room 5508
New York, NY 10112
"Business-Venture Capitalist"

Christian W. E. Haub
2 Paragon Drive
Montvale, NJ 07645
"Business-(CEO) Great A&P Tea"

W. Roger Haughton
601 Montgomery Street
San Francisco, CA 94111
"Business-(CEO) PMI Group"

Richard Haworth
One Haworth Center
Holland, MI 49423
"Business-Haworth, Inc."

Chip Hazard
880 Winter Street
Waltham, MA 02451
"Business-Venture Capitalist"

Austin Hearst
888 - 7th Avenue
New York, NY 10019
"Business- Inheritance (Media)"

David Whitmire Hearst, Jr.
959 - 8th Avenue
New York, NY 10019
"Business- Inheritance (Media)"

George Randolph Hearst
959 - 8th Avenue
New York, NY 10019
"Business- Inheritance (Media)"

William Hearst III
2750 Sand Hill Road
Menlo Park, CA 94025
"Business-Investments (KPCB)"

Donald B. Hebb, Jr.
400 East Pratt Street, Suite 910
Baltimore, MD 21202
"Business-Venture Capitalist"

William F. Hecht
Two North Ninth Street
Allentown, PA 18101
"Business-(CEO) PPL"

Michael Heisley, Sr.
975 Weiland Road
Chicago, IL 60089
"Business-(CEO) WorldPort Communications"

David Helfrich
305 Lytton Avenue
Palo Alto, California 94301
"Business-Venture Capitalist"

Bill Helman
880 Winter Street
Waltham, MA 02451
"Business-Venture Capitalist"

Leona Helmsley
36 Central Park South
New York, NY 10019
"Business-Investments (KPCB)"

Gardner C. Hendrie
20 Custom House Street, Suite 830
Boston, MA 02110
"Business-Venture Capitalist"

Herbert Henkel
200 Chestnut Ridge Road
Woodcliff Lake, NJ 07675
"Business-(CEO) Ingersoll-Rand"

Millionaire Directory   2nd edition

Marvin J. Herb
7400 North Oak Park South
Niles, IL 60714
"Business-Coca-Cola Bottling"

Larissa Herda
10475 Park Meadows Drive
Littleton, CO 80124
"Business-(CEO) Time Warner Telecom"

John B. Hess
1185 Avenue of the Americas
New York, NY 10036
"Business-(CEO) Amerada Hess"

William V. Hickey
Park 80 East
Saddle Brook, NJ 07663
"Business-(CEO) Sealed Air"

Thomas O. Hicks
200 Crescent Center #1600
Dallas, TX 75201
"Business-Leveraged Buyouts"

Richard G. Hickson
P.O. Box 291
Jackson, MS 39205
"Business-(CEO) Trustmark"

Clifford Higgerson
305 Lytton Avenue
Palo Alto, California 94301
"Business-Venture Capitalist"

Walter Higgins III
6100 Neil Road
Reno, NV 89511
"Business-(CEO) Sierra Pacific Resouces"

Allen M. Hill
Courthouse Plaza Southwest
Dayton, OH 45402
"Business-(CEO) DPL"

Richard Hill
4000 North First Street
San Jose, CA 95134
"Business-(CEO) Novellus Systems"

Vernon W. Hill II
1701 Route 70 East
Cherry Hill, NJ 08034
"Business-(CEO) Commerce Bancorp"

Henry Lea Hillman
330 Grant Street
Pittsburg, PA 15219
"Business-Conglomerate"

Glen H. Hiner
One Owens Corning Parkway
Toledo, OH 43659
"Business-(CEO) Owens Corning"

Chuck Hirsch
1000 Second Ave., Ste. 3700
Seattle, WA 98104
"Business-Venture Capitalist"

Laurence E. Hirsch
2728 North Harwood
Dallas, TX 75201
"Business-(CEO) Centex"

Jay Hoag
575 High St., Suite 400
Palo Alto, CA 94301
"Business-Venture Capitalist"

Thomas Hoaglin
Huntington Center
Columbus, OH 43287
"Business-(CEO) Huntington Bancshares"

David C. Hodgson
c/o General Atlantic Partners
Three Pickwick Plaza
Greenwich, CT 06830
"Business-Venture Capitalist"

Millionaire Directory   2nd edition

Bob Hoff
Crosspoint Venture Partners
18552 MacArthur Blvd. Suite 400
Irvine, CA 92612
"Business-Venture Capitalist"

Lewis R. Holding
P.O. Box 27131
Raleigh, NC 27611
"Business-(CEO) First Citizens Bancshares"

Robert Earl Holding
550 East South Temple Street
Salt Lake City, UT 84102
"Business-Gas Stations"

Charles O. Holliday, Jr
1007 Market Street
Wilmington, DE 19898
"Business-(CEO) du pont de Nemours"

B.B. (Ben) Hollingsworth, Jr
950 Echo Lane
Houston, TX 77024
"Business-(CEO) Group 1 Automotive"

Courtney Ross Holst
18 Goodfriend Drive
East Hampton, NY 11937
"Business-Inheritance & Ross School"

Mike Homer
1350 Villa St., Suite 300
Mountain View, CA 94041 USA
"Business-(CEO) Kontiki & Angel Investor"

Van B. Honeycutt
2100 East Grand Avenue
El Segundo, CA 90245
"Business-(CEO) Computer Sciences"

R. David Hoover
10 Longs Peak Drive
Broomfield, CO 80021
"Business-(CEO) Ball"

Basil Horangic
701 N. Brazos St., Suite 1400
Austin, Texas 78701
"Business-Venture Capitalist"

Ralph Horn
P.O. Box 84
Memphis, TN 38101
"Business-(CEO) First Tennessee Natl.)

John R. Horne
455 North Cityfront Plaza Drive
Chicago, IL 60611
"Business-(CEO) Navistar International"

David Hornik
2480 Sand Hill Road, Suite 101
Menlo Park, CA 94025
"Business-Venture Capitalist"

Amos Barr Hostetter, Jr.
The Pilot House, Lewis Wharf
Boston, MA 02110
"Business-Cable Television"

Robert L. Hoverson
One East Fourth Street
Cincinnati, OH 45202
"Business-(CEO) Provident Financial Group"

Matthew D. Howard
525 University Avenue, Suite 800
Palo Alto, CA 94301
"Business-Venture Capitalist"

Jen-Hsun Huang
3535 Monroe Street
Santa Clara, CA 95051
"Business-(CEO) Nvidia"

Stanley Stub Hubbard
3415 University Avenue West
Saint Paul, MN 55114
"Business-Broadcasting"

Millionaire Directory   2nd edition

C. B Hudson
2001 Third Avenue South
Birmingham, AL 35233
"Business-(CEO) Torchmark"

Bradley Wayne Hughes
701 Western Avenue #200
Glendale, CA 91201
"Business-Public Storage, Inc."

David H. Hughes
20 North Orange Avenue
Orlando, FL 32802
"Business-(CEO) Hughes Supply"

H. Wayne Huizenga
450 East Las Olas Blvd. #1500
Fort Lauderdale, FL 33301
"Business-Investments"

Phillip Humann
P.O. Box 4418
Atlanta, GA 30302
"Business-(CEO) SunTrust Banks"

W. Michael Humphreys
Bay Colony Corporate Center
1000 Winter St., Suite 4500
Waltham, MA 02451
"Business-Venture Capitalist"

Ray Lee Hunt
1445 Ross at Field
Dallas, TX 75202
"Business-Oil & Gas"

John C. Hunter III
P.O. Box 66760
St Louis, MO 63166
"Business-(CEO) Solutia"

Jon Meade Huntsman
500 Huntsman Way
Salt Lake City, UT 84108
"Business-Chemicals"

Carl Icahn
100 South Bedford Road
Mount Kisco, NY 10549
"Business-Finance (Investments)"

Martha Robinson Rivers Ingram
4400 Harding Road
Nashville, TN 37205
"Business-Ingram Micro"

Ray Irani
10889 Wilshire Blvd.
Los Angeles, CA 90024
"Business-(CEO) Occidental Petroleum"

Eugene M. Isenberg
515 West Greens Road
Houston, TX 77067
"Business-(CEO) Nabors Industries"

Joseph Ivey
3 Greenway Plaza
Houston, TX 77046
"Business-(CEO) Encompass Services"

Jess Stonestreet Jackson
421 Aviation Blvd.
Santa Rosa, CA 95403
"Business-Wine (Kendall-Jackson)"

Millionaire Directory   2nd edition

Michael J. Jackson
110 Southeast 6th Street
Fort Lauderdale, FL 33301
"Business-(CEO) AutoNation"

Bradley Jacobs
5 Greenwich Office Park
Greenwich, CT 06830
"Business-(CEO) United Rentals"

Irwin Mark Jacobs
5775 Morehouse Drive
San Diego, CA 92121
"Business-(CEO) Qualcomm"

Joseph Dahr Jamail, Jr.
3682 Wilwick Road
Houston, TX 77019
"Business-Lawsuits"

Donald M. James
P.O. Box 385014
Birmingham, AL 35238
"Business-(CEO) Vulcan Materials"

Thomas A. James
P.O. Box 12749
St Petersburg, FL 337
"Business-(CEO) Raymond James Financial"

J. Burgess Jamieson
1600 El Camino Real, Suite. 280
Menlo Park, CA 94025
"Business-Venture Capitalist"

Jim Jannard
One Icon
Foothill Ranch, CA 92610
"Business-Sunglasses (Oakley)"

Kenneth M. Jastrow II
Drawer N
Diboll, TX 75941
"Business-(CEO) Temple-Inland"

C. Bradford Jeffries
1600 El Camino Real, Suite 280
Menlo Park, CA 94025
"Business-Venture Capitalist"

Timothy Jenson
200 Continental Boulevard
El Segundo, CA 90245
"Business-(CEO) Merisel"

Steven Paul Jobs
101 West Cutting Road
Richmond, CA 94804
"Business-Apple Computers"

Jeffrey Joerres
P.O. Box 2053
Milwaukee, WI 53201
"Business-(CEO) Manpower"

Abigail Johnson
82 Devonshire Street
Boston, MA 02109
"Business-Money Manager (Fidelity)"

Amal Johnson
2882 Sand Hill Road, Suite 106
Menlo Park, CA 94025
"Business-Venture Capitalist"

Bobby Ray Johnson
P.O. Box 64910
San Jose, CA 95164
"Business-Foundry Networks"

Charles Bartlett Johnson
777 Mariners Island Blvd.
San Mateo, CA 94404
"Business-(CEO) Franklin Resources"

Edward Crosby Johnson III
82 Devonshire Street
Boston, MA 02109
"Business-Money Manager (Fidelity)"

Millionaire Directory   2nd edition

Joel W. Johnson
1 Hormel Place
Austin, MN 55912
"Business-(CEO) Hormel Foods"

Robert L. Johnson
1900 W. Place N.E.
Washington, DC 20018
"Business-(CEO) Black Entertainment TV"

Rupert Johnson, Jr.
777 Mariners Island Blvd.
San Mateo, CA 94404
"Business-Franklin Resources"

Samuel Curtis Johnson
4815 Lighthouse Drive
Racine, WI 53402
"Business-S.C. Johnson & Son"

Thomas S. Johnson
90 Park Avenue
New York, NY 10016
"Business-(CEO) Green Point Financial"

William R. Johnson
P.O. Box 57
Pittsburgh, PA 15230
"Business-(CEO) HJ Heinz"

John R. Johnston
2480 Sand Hill Road, Suite 101
Menlo Park, CA 94025
"Business-Venture Capitalist"

Howard Jonas
520 Broad Street
Newark, NJ 07102
"Business-(CEO) IDT"

Bradford G. Jones
3000 Sand Hill Rd., Bldg. 2, Suite 290
Menlo Park, CA 94025
"Business-Venture Capitalist"

Carl E. Jones, Jr
P.O. Box 10247
Birmingham, AL 35202
"Business-(CEO) Regions Financial"

D. Paul Jones, Jr
15 South 20th Street
Birmingham, AL 35233
"Business-(CEO) Compass Bancshare"

Jerral (Jerry) W. Jones
One Cowboys Parkway
Irving, TX 75063
"Business-Oil & Gas, Sports Team"

John Jones III
7201 Hamilton Blvd.
Allentown, PA 18195
"Business-(CEO) Air Products & Chemicals"

Blake Jorgensen
c/o Thomas Weisel partners
1 Montgomery Street
San Francisco, CA 94104
"Business-Venture Capitalist"

L. Daniel Jorndt
200 Wilmot Road
Deerfield, IL 60015
"Business-(CEO) Walgreen"

Gregory P. Josefowicz
100 Phoenix Drive
Ann Arbor, MI 48108
"Business-(CEO) Borders"

George Joseph
4484 Wilshire Blvd.
Los Angeles, CA 90010
"Business-Mercury General Corp."

Mary Junck
215 North Main Street
Davenport, IA 52801
"Business-(CEO) Lee Enterprises"

Millionaire Directory 2nd edition

Andrea Jung
1345 Avenue of the Americas
New York, NY 10205
"Business-(CEO) Avon Products"

William G. (Jerry) Jurgensen
One Nationwide Plaza
Columbus, OH 43215
"Business-(CEO) Nationwide Financial Services"

Steve T. Jurvetson
DFJ, 400 Seaport Court, Suite 250
Redwood City, CA 94063
"Business-Venture Capitalist"

Glen Kacher
2750 Sand Hill Rd.
Menlo Park, CA 94025
"Business-Venture Capitalist"

Neil Kadisha
9420 Wilshire Blvd. #400
Beverly Hills, CA 90212
"Business-Omninet Capital"

Robert Kagle
2480 Sand Hill Road, Suite #200
Menlo Park, CA 94025
"Business-Venture Capitalist"

Eugene S. Kahn
611 Olive Street
St Louis, MO 63101
"Business-(CEO) May Dept. Stores"

George B. Kaiser
P.O. Box 2300
Tulsa, OK 74192
"Business-Oil & Gas"

William Kaiser
880 Winter Street
Waltham, MA 02451
"Business-Venture Capitalist"

Gary Kalbach
2884 Sand Hill Road, Suite 121
Menlo Park, CA 94025
"Business-Venture Capitalist"

David Kalkbrenner
2860 West Bayshore Road
Palo Alto, CA 94303
"Business-(CEO) Greater Bay Bancorp"

John Adam Kanas
275 Broad Hollow Road
Melville, NY 11747
"Business-(CEO) North Fork Bancorp"

Peter R. Kann
200 Liberty Street
New York, NY 10281
"Business-(CEO) Dow Jones"

Bruce E. Karatz
10990 Wilshire Blvd.
Los Angeles, CA 90024
"Business-(CEO) KB Homes"

Peter Karmanos, Jr.
31440 Northwestern Highway
Farmington Hills, MI 48334
"Business-(CEO) Compuware"

Jeffrey Katzenberg
100 Flower Street
Glendale, CA 91201
"Business-Entertainment"

Herbert Kelleher
P.O. Box 36611
Dallas, TX 75235
"Business-(CEO) Southwest Airlines"

Millionaire Directory   2nd edition

Peter R. Kellogg
120 Broadway, Libby 6
New York, NY 10271
"Business-Spear, Leeds & Kellogg"

William Kellogg
N56 West 17000 Ridgewood Dr.
Menomonee, WI 53051
"Business-Retail"

Edward Kelly III
P.O. Box 1477
Baltimore, MD 21203
"Business-(CEO) Mercantile Bankshares"

James P. Kelly
55 Glenlake Parkway NE
Atlanta, GA 30328
"Business-(CEO) United Parcel Services"

David W. Kemper
P.O. Box 13686
Kansas City, MO 64199
"Business-(CEO) Commerce Bancshares"

R. Crosby Kemper
P.O. Box 419226
Kansas City, MO 64141
"Business-(CEO) UMB Financial"

Parker S. Kennedy
1 First American Way
Santa Ana, CA 92707
"Business-(CEO) First American"

Jerald L. Kent
12444 Powerscourt Drive
St Louis, MO 63131
"Business-(CEO) Charter Communications"

Kirk Kerkorian
3799 Las Vegas Blvd.
Las vegas, NV 89109
"Business-Hotel & Casinos (MGM Grand)"

James H. Keyes
P.O. Box 591
Milwaukee, WI 53201
"Business-(CEO) Johnson Controls"

James W. Keyes
P.O. Box 711
Dallas, TX 75221
"Business-(CEO) 7-Eleven"

Richard L. Keyser
100 Grainger Parkway
Lake Forest, IL 60045
"Business-(CEO) WW Grainger"

Vinod Khosla
2750 Sand Hill Road
Menlo Park, CA 94025
"Business-Venture Capitalist"

Peter J. Kight
4411 East Jones Bridge Road
Norcross, GA 30092
"Business-(CEO) CheckFree"

Kerry Killinger
1201 Third Avenue
Seattle, WA 98101
"Business- (CEO) Washington Mutual"

James M. Kilts
Prudential Tower Building
Boston, MA 02199
"Business-(CEO) Gillette"

James Kim
1345 Enterprise Drive
West Chester, PA 19380
"Business-Microchips"

Rick Kimball
575 High St., Suite 400
Palo Alto, CA 94301
"Business-Venture Capitalist"

Millionaire Directory   2nd edition

Sidney Kimmel
250 Rittenhouse Circle
Bristol, PA 19007
"Business-(CEO) Jones Apparel Group"

Mark T. Kimura
11150 Santa Monica Blvd. Suite 1200
Los Angeles, CA 90025
"Business-Venture Capitalist"

Richard D. Kinder
500 Dallas Street #1000
Houston, TX 77002
"Business-(CEO) Kinder Morgan"

Steve Kirsch
1010 Rincon Circle
San Jose, CA 95131
"Business-(CEO) Propel Corp."

Alan Kirshner
4521 Highwoods Parkway
Glen Allen, VA 23060
"Business-(CEO) Markel"

Bob Kitt
c/o Thomas Weisel partners
1 Montgomery Street
San Francisco, CA 94104
"Business-Venture Capitalist"

John A. Klein
850 Main Street
Bridgeport, CT 06601
"Business-(CEO) People's Bank"

Lowry Kline
P.O. Box 723040
Atlanta, GA 31139
"Business-(CEO) Coca-Cola Enterprises"

John Werner Kluge
One Meadowland Plaza
East Rutherford, NJ 07073
"Business-Metromedia"

J. Barclay Knapp
110 East 59th Street
New York, NY 10022
"Business-(CEO) NTL"

Brian Knez
27 Boylston Street
Chestnut Hill, MA 02467
"Business-(CEO) Harcourt General"

Philip H. Knight
One Bowerman Drive
Beaverton, OR 97005
"Business-(CEO) Nike"

Charles DeGanahl Koch
P.O. Box 2256
4111 East 37th Street North
Wichita, KS 67220
"Business-Oil Services"

Charles John Koch
1215 Superior Avenue
Cleveland, OH 44114
"Business-(CEO) Charter One Financial"

David Hamilton Koch
677 Madison Avenue, 22nd floor
New York, N Y 10021
"Business-Oil Services"

William Ingraham Koch
1601 Forum Place
West Plam Beach, FL 33401
"Business-Inheritance (Oil Services)"

Brad Koenig
c/o Goldman Sachs
2765 Sand Hill Road
Menlo Park, CA 94025
"Business-Banker"

Richard Jay Kogan
2000 Galloping Hill Road
Kenilworth, NJ 07033
"Business-CEO (Schering-Plough)"

41

Millionaire Directory 2nd edition

Herbert Kohler
444 Highland Drive
Kohler, WI 53044
"Business-Plumbing Fixture"

Robert J. Kohlhepp
P.O. Box 625737
Cincinnati, OH 45262
"Business-(CEO) Cintas"

David Komansky
World Financial Center
New York, NY 10281
"Business-(CEO) Merrill Lynch"

Paul Koontz
70 Willow Rd, Suite 200
Menlo Park, CA 94025
"Business-Venture Capitalist"

Allen H. Koranda
55th Street & Holmes Avenue
Clarendon Hills, IL 60514
Business-(CEO) MAF Bancorp."

Richard Kovacevich
420 Montgomery Street
San Francisco, CA 94163
"Business- (CEO) Wells Fargo"

Bruce Kovner
667 Madison Avenue, 10th floor
New York, NY 10021
"Business-Money Manager"

Michael T. Kowalski
727 Fifth Avenue
New York, NY 10022
"Business-(CEO) Tiffany"

Harry Jansen Kraemer, Jr
One Baxter Parkway
Deerfield, IL 60015
"Business-(CEO) Baxter International"

Richard C. Kramlich
2490 Sand Hill Road
Menlo Park, CA 94025
"Business-Venture Capitalist"

Michical Krasny
200 N. Milwaukee Avenue
Vernon Hills, IL 60061
"Business-Computer Discounts "

Steven Krausz
2180 San Hill Road, Suite #300
Menlo Park, CA 94025
"Business-Venture Capitalist"

Henry R. Kravis
9 West 57th Street
New York, NY 10019
"Business-Leveraged Buyouts"

Frederick A. Krehbiel
2222 Wellington Court
Lisle, IL 60532-1682
"Business-(CEO) Molex"

John Hammond Krehbiel
2222 Wellington Avenue
Lisle, IL 60332
"Business-Molex, Inc."

Kent Kresa
1840 Century Park East
Los Angeles, CA 90067
"Business-(CEO) Northrop Grumman"

Scott Kriens
P.O. Box 3786
Sunnyvale, CA 94088
"Business-(CEO) Juniper Networks"

Joan Kroc
8939 Villa la Jolla Drive
LaJolla, CA 92037
"Business-Inheritance (McDonald)"

Millionaire Directory   2nd edition

Sanjay Kumar
One Computer Associates Plaza
Islandia, NY 11749
"Business-(CEO) Computer Associates"

Mark Kvamme
3000 Sand Hill Road
Bldg. 4, Suite 180
Menlo Park, CA 94025
"Business-Venture Capitalist"

David Kyle
P.O. Box 871
Tulsa, OK 74102
"Business-(CEO) Oneok"

Alan Lacy
3333 Beverly Road
Hoffman Estates, IL 60179
"Business-(CEO) Sears, Roebuck"

David Ladd
2800 Sand Hill Road, Suite 250
Menlo Park, CA 94025
"Business-Venture Capitalist"

Alan Lafley
One Procter & Gamble Plaza
Cincinnati, OH 45202
"Business-(CEO) Procter & Gamble"

Pierre Lamond
3000 Sand Hill Road
Bldg. 4, Suite 180
Menlo Park, CA 94025
"Business-Venture Capitalist"

Ann Lamont
525 University Avenue, Suite 1300
Palo Alto, CA 94301
"Business-Venture Capitalist"

Sean P. Lance
4560 Horton Street
Emeryville, CA 94608
"Business-(CEO) Chiron"

Amnon Landan
1325 Borregas Avenue
Sunnyvale, CA 94089
"Business-(CEO) Mercury Interactive"

Michel Landel
9801 Washingtonian Blvd.
Gaithersburg, MD 20878
"Business-(CEO) Sodexho Marriott"

Robert Lane
One John Deere Place
Moline, IL 61265
"Business-(CEO) Deere & Company"

Bill Lanfri
428 University Avenue
Palo Alto, CA 94301
"Business-Venture Capitalist"

Fred Langhammer
767 Fifth Avenue
New York, NY 10153
"Business-(CEO) Estee Lauder"

Kenneth Langone
375 park Avenue #2205
New York, NY 10152
"Business-Investments"

J. Terrence Lanni
3600 Las Vegas Blvd. South
Las Vegas, NV 89109
"Business-(CEO) MGM Mirage"

William J. Lansing
c/o General Atlantic Partners
Three Pickwick Plaza
Greenwich, CT 06830
"Business-Venture Capitalist"

Millionaire Directory   2nd edition

Randall W. Larrimore
2200 East Golf Road
Des Plaines, IL 60016
"Business-(CEO) United Stationers"

Ralph S. Larsen
One Johnson & Johnson Plaza
New Brunswick, NJ 08933
"Business- (CEO) Johnson & Johnson"

Phillip Lassiter
One State Street Plaza
New York, NY 10004
"Business- (CEO) Ambac Financial Group"

Pat Latterell
2494 Sand Hill Road, Suite 200
Menlo Park, CA 94025
"Business-Venture Capitalist"

Leonard Alan Lauder
765 - 5th Avenue
New York, NY 10153
"Business-Estee Lauder"

Ronald Steven Lauder
765 - 5th Avenue
New York, NY 10153
"Business-Estee Lauder"

Ralph Lauren
650 Madison Avenue
New York, NY 10022
"Business-Polo"

Bruce R. Lauritzen
1 First National Center
Omaha, NE 68102
"Business-(CEO) First National Nebraska"

Warren T. Lazarow
c/o Brobeck, Phleger & Harrison
Two Embarcadero Place, 2200 Geng Road
Palo Alto, CA 94303
"Professional-Lawyer"

Douglas W. Leatherdale
385 Washington Street
St Paul, MN 55102
"Business-(CEO) St. Paul Companies"

Raymond W. LeBoeuf
One PPG Place
Pittsburgh, PA 15272
"Business-(CEO) PPG Industries"

Bennett S. LeBow
100 Southeast 2nd Street
Miami, FL 33131
"Business-(CEO) Vector Group"

Charles Lee
1095 Avenue of the Americas
New York, NY 10036
"Business-(CEO) Verizon Communications"

Joe R. Lee
5900 Lake Ellenor Drive
Orlando, FL 3280
Business-(CEO) Darden Restaurants"

Samuel Jayson Lefrak
97 - 77 Queens Blvd.
Rego Park, NY 11374
"Business-Real Estate"

Joseph H. Lemieux
One SeaGate
Toledo, OH 43666
"Business-(CEO) Owens-Illinois"

Harold Fitzgerald Lenfest
1332 Enterprise Drive
West Chester, PA 19380
"Business-Microchips"

Richard Lenny
P.O. Box 810
Hershey, PA 17033
"Business-(CEO) Hershey Foods"

Millionaire Directory   2nd edition

J. Wayne Leonard
P.O. Box 61000
New Orleans, LA 70161
Business-(CEO) Entergy"

Douglas Leone
3000 Sand Hill Road
Bldg. 4, Suite 180
Menlo Park, CA 94025
"Business-Venture Capitalist"

Alfred Lerner
19000 South Park Blvd.
Cleveland, OH 44122
"Business-Banks-(CEO) MBNA"

David Lesar
3600 Lincoln Plaza
Dallas, TX 75201
Business-(CEO) Halliburton"

R. Steve Letbetter
P.O. Box 4567
Houston, TX 77210
"Business-(CEO) Reliant Energy"

Gerald M. Levin
22000 AOL Way
Dulles, VA 20166
"Business-(CEO) AOL-Time Warner"

Mark J. Levin
75 Sidney Street
Cambridge, MA 02139
"Business-(CEO) Millennium Pharm"

Howard R. Levine
P.O. Box 1017
Charlotte, NC 28201
"Business-(CEO) Family Dollar Stores"

Salomon Levis
1159 Franklin D Roosevelt Ave
San Juan, PR 00920
"Business-(CEO) Doral Financial"

Arthur Levinson
1 DNA Way
South San Francisco, CA 94080
"Business-(CEO) Genentech"

Frank Levinson
1308 Moffett Park Drive
Sunnyvale, CA 94089
"Business-Fiber Optics (Finisar)"

Leon Levy
280 Park Avenue, 21st Floor, W.
New York, NY 10015
"Business-Money Manager"

Kenneth Lewis
Corporate Center
Charlotte, NC 28255
"Business-(CEO) Bank of America"

Merle D. Lewis
125 South Dakota Avenue
Sioux Falls, SD 57104
"Business-(CEO) NorthWestern"

Peter Benjamin Lewis
6300 Wilson Mills Road
Cleveland, OH 44143
"Business-Progressive Corp."

Russell T. Lewis
229 West 43rd Street
New York, NY 10036
"Business-(CEO) New York Times"

Edward Liddy
2775 Sanders Road
Northbrook, IL 60062
"Business-(CEO) AllState"

David Lilley
5 Garret Mountain Plaza
West Paterson, NJ 07424
"Business-(CEO) Cytec Industries"

Millionaire Directory   2nd edition

George L. Lindemann
504 Lavaca, #800
Austin, TX 78701
"Business- Investments (Southern Union)"

Carl Henry Lindner, Jr.
One East Fourth Street
Cincinnati, OH 45202
"Business-(CEO) American Fanciainl Group"

Mike Linnert
575 High St., Suite 400
Palo Alto, CA 94301
"Business-Venture Capitalist"

Gerald H. Lipkin
1455 Valley Road
Wayne, NJ 07470
"Business-(CEO) Valley National Bancorp"

Bob Lisbonne
2500 Sand Hill Road, Suite 200
Menlo Park, CA 94025
"Business-Venture Capitalist"

Donald Listwin
800 Chesapeake Drive
Redwood City, CA 94063
"Business-(CEO) Openwave Systems"

Edmund Wattis Littlefield
P.O. Box 3001
Lancaster, PA 17604
"Business-(CEO) Armstrong Holding"

John Loose
One Riverfront Plaza
Corning, NY 14831
"Business-(CEO) Corning"

Jeffrey Lorberbaum
P.O. Box 12069
Calhoun, GA 30703
"Business-(CEO) Mohawk Industries"

Albert Lord
11600 Sallie Mae Drive
Reston, VA 20193
"Business-(CEO) USA Education"

Robert E. Lowder
One Commerce Street
Montgomery, AL 36104
"Business-(CEO) Colonial BancGroup"

Kenneth Lowe
P.O. Box 5380
Cincinnati, OH 45201
"Business-(CEO) EW Scripps"

George Lucas
P.O. Box 2009
San Rafael, CA 94912
"Business-Microchips"

Edward J. Ludwig
1 Becton Drive
Franklin Lakes, NJ 07417
"Business-(CEO) Becton Dickinson"

John A. Luke, Jr
299 Park Avenue
New York, NY 10171
"Business-(CEO) Westvaco"

Joseph W. Luter III
200 Commerce Street
Smithfield, VA 23430
"Business-(CEO) Smithfield Foods"

Stanley A. Lybarger
P.O. Box 2300
Tulsa, OK 74192
"Business-(CEO) BOK Financial"

Millionaire Directory 2nd edition

Frank Macher
26555 Northwestern Highway
Southfield, MI 48034
"Business-(CEO) Federal-Mogul"

Frank T. MacInnis
101 Merritt Seven
Norwalk, CT 06851
"Business-(CEO) Emcor Group"

John W. Madigan
435 North Michigan Avenue
Chicago, IL 60611
"Business-(CEO) Tribune"

Maggie Hardy Magerko
84 Lumber Co., Route 519
Eightyfour, PA 15330
"Business-Lumber"

Joseph Magliochetti
P.O. Box 1000
Toledo, OH 43697
"Business-(CEO) Dana"

Gary Magness
P.O. Box 190
Platteville, CO 80651
"Business-Inheritance (Cable TV)"

Sharon Magness
P.O. Box 190
Platteville, CO 80651
"Business-Inheritance (Cable TV)"

David Maguire
2835 Kemet Way
Simpsonville, SC 29681
"Business-(CEO) Kemet"

Thomas Mac Mahon
358 South Main Street
Burlington, NC 27215
"Business-(CEO) Laboratory Corp. of Amer."

Timothy Main
10560 Ninth Street North
St Petersburg, FL 33716
"Business-(CEO) Jabil Circuit"

John C. Malone
9197 South Peoria Street
Englewood, CO 80112
"Business-Cable Television"

Wallace D. Malone, Jr
P.O. Box 2554
Birmingham, AL 35290
"Business-(CEO) South Trust"

Joseph L. Mancino
One Jericho Plaza
Jericho, NY 11753
"Business-(CEO) Roslyn Bancorp"

John Mandile
20 Custom House Street, Suite 830
Boston, MA 02110
"Business-Venture Capitalist"

Alfred Mann
P.O. Box 905
Valencia, CA 91380
"Business-Investments"

James L. Mann
1285 Drummers Lane
Wayne, PA 19087
"Business-(CEO) SunGard Data Systems"

Richard Alexander Manoogian
21001 Van Born Road
Taylor, MI 48180
"Business-(CEO) Masco Corp."

Millionaire Directory 2nd edition

Bernard Marcus
2455 Paces Ferry Road S.E.
Atlanta, GA 30339
"Business-Home Depot"

Andrew Marcuvitz
Bay Colony Corporate Center
1000 Winter St., Suite 4500
Waltham, MA 02451
"Business-Venture Capitalist"

Ernest Mario
P.O. Box 7210
Mountain View, CA 94039
Business-(CEO) ALZA"

Reuben Mark
300 Park Avenue
New York, NY 10022
"Business-(CEO) Colgate-Palmolive"

William L. Marks
228 St Charles Avenue
New Orleans, LA 70130
"Business-(CEO) Whitney Holding"

David F. Marquardt
2480 Sand Hill Road, Suite 101
Menlo Park, CA 94025
"Business-Venture Capitalist"

John Willard Marriott, Jr.
One Marriott Drive
Washington, DC 20058
"Business-(CEO) Marriott Hotels"

Forrest Edward Mars, Jr.
6885 Elm Street
McLean, VA 22101
"Business-Candy"

Jacqueline Badger Mars
6885 Elm Street
McLean, VA 22101
"Business-Candy"

John Franklyn Mars
6885 Elm Street
McLean, VA 22101
"Business-Candy"

Ron Marshall
7600 France Avenue S
Edina, MN 55435
"Business-(CEO) Nash Finch"

Thomas Marsico
1200 - 17th Street #1300
Denver, CO 80202
"Business-Money Manager"

Hugh Martin
166 Baypointe Parkway
San Jose, CA 95134
"Business-(CEO) ONI Systems"

Peter M. Martin
114 East Lexington Street
Baltimore, MD 21202
"Business-(CEO) Provident Bankshares"

R. Brad Martin
750 Lakeshore Parkway
Birmingham, AL 35211
"Business-(CEO) Saks"

Robert E. Martini
4000 Metropolitan Drive
Orange, CA 92868
"Business-(CEO) Bergen Brunswig"

Raymond Mason
100 Light Street
Baltimore, MD 21202
"Business-(CEO) Legg Mason"

Edgar Masri
Bay Colony Corporate Center
1000 Winter St., Suite 4500
Waltham, MA 02451
"Business-Venture Capitalist"

Millionaire Directory   2nd edition

Clayton Lee Mathile
P.O. Box 13615
Dayton, OH 45413
"Business-Iams Petfood"

Thomas J. May
800 Boylston Street
Boston, MA 02199
"Business-(CEO) NStar"

L. Lowry Mays
200 East Basse Road
San Antonio, TX 78209
"Business-(CEO) Clear Channel Communs."

Greg McAdoo
3000 Sand Hill Road, Bldg. 4, Suite 180
Menlo Park, CA 94025
"Business-Venture Capitalist"

Edward L. McCall
11150 Santa Monica Blvd. Suite 1200
Los Angeles, CA 90025
"Business-Venture Capitalist"

Michael B. McCallister
500 West Main Street
Louisville, KY 40202
"Business-(CEO) Humana"

Henry McCance
880 Winter Street
Waltham, MA 02451
"Business-Venture Capitalist"

Bill McCanless
P.O. Box 1330
Salisbury, NC 28145
"Business-(CEO) Delhaize America"

Bruce R. McCaw
1501 Quail Street #103
Newport Beach, CA 92660
"Business-Telecom"

Craig McCaw
1445 - 120 Avenue N.E.
Belleveue, WA 98005
"Business-Telecom"

John Elroy McCaw, Jr.
800 Griffiths Way
Vancouver, BC CANADA V6B 6G1
"Business-Telecom"

W Alan McCollough
9950 Mayland Drive
Richmond, VA 23233
"Business-(CEO) Circuit City"

Billy Joe "Red" McCombs
9520 Viking Drive
Eden Prairie, MN 55344
"Business-Auto Sales & Sports Team"

Douglas McCorkindale
1100 Wilson Blvd.
Arlington, VA 22234
"Business- (CEO) Gannett"

Mark McCormack
1360 East 9th Street #100
Cleveland, OH 44114
"Business-Sports Management"

Rob McCormack
2750 Sand Hill Rd.
Menlo Park, CA 94025
"Business-Venture Capitalist"

William T. McCormick, Jr
330 Town Center Drive
Dearborn, MI 48126
"Business-(CEO) CMS Energy"

David C. McCourt
105 Carnegie Center
Princeton, NJ 08540
"Business-CEO (RCN)"

Millionaire Directory   2nd edition

James McDonald
5030 Sugarloaf Parkway
Lawrenceville, GA 30044
"Business-CEO (Scientific Atlanta)"

Mackey J. McDonald
678 Green Valley Road
Greensboro, NC 27408
"Business-(CEO) VF Corp."

Stephen D. McDonald
100 Wall Street
New York, NY 10005
"Business-CEO (TD Waterhouse Group)"

Thomas McDonnell
333 West 11th Street
Kansas City, MO 64105
"Business-CEO (DST Systems)"

Duane C. McDougall
300 SW Fifth Avenue
Portland, OR 97201
"Business-(CEO) Willamette Industries"

Michael McGavick
Safeco Plaza
Seattle, WA 98185
"Business-(CEO) Safeco"

W. Patrick McGinnis
One Checkerboard Square
St Louis, MO 63164
"Business-(CEO) Ralston Purina"

Patrick Joseph McGovern
One Exeter Plaza, 15th Floor
Boston, MA 02116
"Business-Publishing"

Eugene R. McGrath
4 Irving Place
New York, NY 10003
"Business-(CEO) Consolidated Edison"

Harold McGraw III
1221 Avenue of the Americas
New York, NY 10020
"Business-(CEO) McGraw-Hill Company"

Martin G. McGuinn
One Mellon Center
Pittsburgh, PA 15258
"Business- (CEO) Mellon Financial"

William W. McGuire
9900 Bren Road East
Minnetonka, MN 55343
"Business-(CEO) UnitedHealth Group"

James A. McIntyre
2020 Santa Monica Boulevard
Santa Monica, CA 90404
"Business-(CEO) Fremont General"

Andrew McKelvey
TMP, 622 Third Avenue, 39th Floor
New York, NY 10017
"Business-(CEO) TMP Worldwide"

Henry McKinnell
235 East 42nd Street
New York, NY 10017
"Business-(CEO) Pfizer"

Robert Drayton McLane, Jr.
P.O. Box 6115
Temple, TX 76503
"Business-Walmart"

Jim McLean
305 Lytton Avenue
Palo Alto, California 94301
"Business-Venture Capitalist"

Clark E. McLeod
P.O. Box 3177
Cedar Rapids, IA 52406
"Business-(CEO) McLeodUSA"

Millionaire Directory 2nd edition

Vincent K. McMahon
1241 East Main Street
Stanford, CT 06902
"Entertainment-Sports (Pro wrestling)"

C. Steven McMillan
Three First National Plaza
Chicago, IL 60602
Business-(CEO) Sara Lee"

Amos R. McMullian
1919 Flowers Circle
Thomasville, GA 31757
"Business-(CEO) Flowers Foods"

Robert McNair
711 Louisiana, 33rd Floor
Houston, TX 72002
"Business-Energy"

Roger McNamee
2750 Sand Hill Rd.
Menlo Park, CA 94025
"Business-Venture Capitalist"

Scott G. McNealy
901 San Antonio Road
Palo Alto, CA 94303
"Business-Sun MicroSystems"

Corbin A. McNeill, Jr
P.O. Box A-3005
Chicago, IL 60690
"Business-(CEO) Exelon"

W. James McNerney, Jr
3M Center
St Paul, MN 55144
"Business-(CEO) 3M-Minnesota Mining & Mfg."

Shailesh Mehta
201 Mission Street
San Francisco, CA 94105
"Business-(CEO) Providian Financial"

John R. Menard, Jr.
4777 Menard Drive
Eau Claire, WI 54703
"Business-Home Improvement Centers"

Debby Meredith
2775 Sand Hill Road, Suite 240
Menlo Park, CA 94025
"Business-Venture Capitalist"

Stan Meresman
575 High St., Suite 400
Palo Alto, CA 94301
"Business-Venture Capitalist"

Zac Merriman
2750 Sand Hill Rd.
Menlo Park, CA 94025
"Business-Venture Capitalist"

Harold Messmer Jr
2884 Sand Hill Road
Menlo Park, CA 94025
"Business-(CEO) Robert Half International"

Henry Meyer III
127 Public Square
Cleveland, OH 44114
"Business-(CEO) KeyCorp"

James Meyer
P.O. Box 8700
Grand Rapids, MI 49518
"Business-(CEO) Spartan Stores"

Morton Meyerson
3401 Armstrong Ave
Dallas, Texas 75205
"Business-Venture Capitalist"

Ravi Mhatre
2882 Sand Hill Road, Suite 106
Menlo Park, CA 94025
"Business-Venture Capitalist"

Millionaire Directory   2nd edition

Gary G. Michael
P.O. Box 20
Boise, ID 83726
"Business-(CEO) Albertson's"

Michael Roberts Milken
4543 Tara Drive
Encino, CA 91436
"Business-Financier"

Dane A. Miller
56 East Bell Drive
Warsaw, IN 46581
"Business-(CEO) Biomet"

Eugene Miller
500 Woodward Avenue
Detroit, MI 48226
"Business-(CEO) Comerica"

Robert Miller
P.O. Box 3165
Harrisburg, PA 17105
"Business-(CEO) Rite Aid"

Stuart A. Miller
700 North West 107th Avenue
Miami, FL 33172
"Business-(CEO) Lennar"

Ted B. Miller, Jr
510 Bering Drive
Houston, TX 77057
"Business-(CEO) Crown Castle International"

Roger Milliken
P.O. Box 1926
Spartanburg, SC 29304
"Business-Textiles"

Peter Mills
3000 Alpine Road
Menlo Park, CA 94028
"Business-Venture Capitalist"

G. Gilmer Minor III
P.O. Box 27626
Richmond, VA 23261
"Business-(CEO) Owens & Minor"

George Phydias Mitchell
P.O. Box 4000
The Woodlands, TX 77387
"Business-(CEO) Mitchell Energy"

Venkat Mohan
525 University Avenue, Suite 800
Palo Alto, CA 94301
"Business-Venture Capitalist"

R. Lawrence Montgomery
N56 W17000 Ridgewood Drive
Menomonee Falls, WI 53051
"Business-(CEO) Kohl's"

Robert L. Moody
One Moody Plaza
Galveston, TX 77550
Business-(CEO) American National"

Geoffrey Moore
2775 Sand Hill Road, Suite 240
Menlo Park, CA 94025
"Business-Venture Capitalist"

Gordon Earle Moore
2200 Mission College Blvd.
Santa Clara, CA 95054
"Business-Intel"

Jackson Moore
P.O. Box 387
Memphis, TN 38147
"Business-(CEO) Union Planters"

Steven E. Moore
P.O. Box 321
Oklahoma City, OK 73101
"Business-(CEO) OGE Energy"

Millionaire Directory 2nd edition

Steven W. Moore
11150 Santa Monica Blvd. Suite 1200
Los Angeles, CA 90025
"Business-Venture Capitalist"

James Martin Moran
100 NW 12th Avenue
Dearfield Beach, FL 33442
"Business-Auto Distributor"

Michael R. Moran
3500 Lacey Road
Downers Grove, IL 60515
"Business-(CEO) Spiegel"

William Morean
10560 North 9th Street
St. Petersburg, FL 33116
"Business-Manufacturing"

Allen Morgan
2800 Sand Hill Road, Suite 250
Menlo Park, CA 94025
"Business-Venture Capitalist"

Cristina Morgan
c/o J.P. Morgan H&Q
1 Bush St.
San Francisco, CA 94104
"Business-Banker"

James C. Morgan
3050 Bowers Avenue
Santa Clara, CA 95054
"Business-(CEO) Applied Materials"

John P. Morgridge
170 West Tas Man Drive
San Jose, CA 95134
"Business-Cisco Systems"

Takahiro Moriguchi
400 California Street
San Francisco, CA 94104
"Business-(CEO) UnionBanCal"

Michael Moritz
3000 Sand Hill Rd., Bldg. 4, Suite. 280
Menlo Park, CA 94025
"Business-Venture Capitalist"

Michael G. Morris
P.O. Box 270
Hartford, CT 06141
"Business-(CEO) Northeast Utilities"

Peter T. Morris
2490 Sand Hill Road
Menlo Park, CA 94025
"Business-Venture Capitalist"

William Charles Morris
c/o J&W Seligman & Co., Inc.
100 Park Avenue
New York, NY 10019
"Business-Money Management"

Robert S. Morrison
P.O. Box 049001
Chicago, IL 60604
"Business-(CEO) Quaker Oats"

Lawrence Mosner
P.O. Box 64235
St Paul, MN 55164
"Business-(CEO) Deluxe"

David Mott
35 West Watkins Mill Road
Gaithersburg, MD 20878
"Business-(CEO) MedImmune"

Angelo R. Mozilo
4500 Park Granada Blvd.
Calabasas, CA 91302
"Business-(CEO) Countrywide Credit"

Charles W. Mueller
P.O. Box 66149
St Louis, MO 63166
"Business-(CEO) Ameren"

Millionaire Directory   2nd edition

James Mullen
14 Cambridge Center
Cambridge, MA 02142
"Business-(CEO) Biogen"

Leo F. Mullin
P.O. Box 20706
Atlanta, GA 30320
"Business-(CEO) Delta Air Lines"

James Mulva
Phillips Building
Bartlesville, OK 74004
"Business-(CEO) Phillips Petroleum"

Leslie M. Muma
255 Fiserv Drive
Brookfield, WI 53045
"Business-(CEO) Fiserv"

John Mumford
The Pioneer Hotel Building
2925 Woodside Road
Woodside, CA 94062
"Business-Venture Capitalist"

Charles Munger
1440 Kiewit Plaza
Omaha, NE 68131
"Business-Investments"

David Howard Murdock
31365 Oak Crest Drive
Westlake Village, CA 91361
"Business-(CEO) Dole Food"

Keith Rupert Murdoch
1211 Avenue of the Americas, 3rd Floor
New York, NY 10036
"Business-Media (Publishing)"

Terrence Murray
100 Federal Street
Boston, MA 02110
"Business-(CEO) FleetBoston Financial"

A. Maurice Myers
1001 Fannin
Houston, TX 77002
"Business-(CEO) Waste Management"

Drayton Nabers, Jr
P.O. Box 2606
Birmingham, AL 35202
"Business-(CEO) Protective Life"

Joseph P. Nacchio
1801 California Street
Denver, CO 80202
"Business-(CEO) Quest Communications"

Robert Nardelli
2455 Paces Ferry Road
Atlanta, GA 30339
"Business-(CEO) Home Depot"

Philip M. Neal
150 North Orange Grove Blvd
Pasadena, CA 91103
"Business-(CEO) Avery Dennison"

Gary L. Neale
801 East 86th Avenue
Merrillville, IN 46410
"Business-(CEO) Ni Source"

Robert Neil
1400 Lake Hearn Drive
Atlanta, GA 30319
"Business-(CEO) Cox Radio"

Kenneth T. Neilson
1000 MacArthur Boulevard
Mahwah, NJ 07430
"Business-(CEO) Hudson United Bancorp"

Millionaire Directory 2nd edition

Seth Neiman
The Pioneer Hotel Building
2925 Woodside Road
Woodside, CA 94062
"Business-Venture Capitalist"

Bruce Nelson
2200 Old Germantown Road
Delray Beach, FL 33445
"Business-(CEO) Office Depot"

Marilyn Carlson Nelson
P.O. Box 59159
Minneapolis, MN 55459
"Business-Travel Services"

Arnold M. Nemirow
P.O. Box 1028
Greenville, SC 29602
"Business-CEO (Bowater)"

Patrick H. Nettles
1201 Winterson Road
Linthicum, MD 21090
"Business-(CEO) Ciena"

Chuck Newhall
1119 St. Paul Street
Baltimore, MD 21202
"Business-Venture Capitalist"

Donald E. Newhouse
950 Fingerboard Road
Staten Island, NY 10305
"Business-Media (Publishing)"

Samuel I. Newhouse, Jr.
950 Fingerboard Road
Staten Island, NY 10305
"Business-Media (Publishing)"

Henry Nicholas, III
16215 Alton Parkway
Irvine, CA 92618
"Business-(CEO) Broadcom"

J. Larry Nichols
20 North Broadway
Oklahoma City, OK 73102
"Business-(CEO) Devon Energy"

Peter M. Nicholas
One Boston Scientific Place
Natick, MA 01760
"Business-Medical Devices"

Peter Nieh
2882 Sand Hill Road, Suite 106
Menlo Park, CA 94025
"Business-Venture Capitalist"

Matthew Nimetz
c/o General Atlantic Partners
Three Pickwick Plaza
Greenwich, CT 06830
"Business-Venture Capitalist"

Koichi Nishimura
847 Gibraltar Drive
Milpitas, CA 95035
"Business-(CEO) Solectron"

Dennis E. Nixon
1200 San Bernardo Avenue
Laredo, TX 78042
"Business-(CEO) International Bancshares"

Alan J. Noia
10435 Downsville Pike
Hagerstown, MD 21740
"Business-(CEO) Allegheny Energy"

Blake Nordstrom
1617 Sixth Avenue
Seattle, WA 98101
"Business-(CEO) Nordstrom"

Richard C. Notebaert
4951 Indiana Avenue
Lisle, IL 60532
"Business-(CEO) Tellabs"

Millionaire Directory   2nd edition

David C. Novak
1441 Gardiner Lane
Louisville, KY 40213
"Business-(CEO) Tricon Global Restaurant"

Donna Novitsky
2775 Sand Hill Road, Suite 240
Menlo Park, CA 94025
"Business-Venture Capitalist"

John J. Nugent
P.O. Box 9601
Natick, MA 01760
"Business-(CEO) BJ's Wholesale Club"

Lars Nyberg
1700 South Patterson Blvd.
Dayton, OH 45479
"Business-(CEO) NCR"

Erle A. Nye
1601 Bryan Street
Dallas, TX 75201
"Business-(CEO) TXU"

John F O'Brien
440 Lincoln Street
Worcester, MA 01653
"Business-(CEO) Allmerica Financial"

Judith Mayer O'Brien
855 Maude Avenue
Mountain View, CA 94043
"Professional-Venture Capitalist/Lawyer"

James E. O'Connor
110 SE Sixth Street
Fort Lauderdale, FL 33301
"Business-(CEO) Republic Services"

Steve Odland
P.O. Box 2198
Memphis, TN 38101
"Business-(CEO) AutoZone"

James Oelschlager
3875 Embassy Parkway #250
Akron, OH 44333
"Business-Money Manager"

Dean R. O'Hare
P.O. Box 1615
Warren, NJ 07061
"Business-(CEO) Chubb"

Ed Olkkola
701 N. Brazos St., Suite 1400
Austin, Texas 78701
"Business-Venture Capitalist"

Thomas O'Malley
72 Cummings Point Road
Stamford, CT 06902
"Business-(CEO) Tosco"

Robert P. O'Meara
300 Park Blvd.
Itasca, IL 60143
"Business-(CEO) First Midwest Bancorp"

Pierre Omidyar
2125 Hamilton Avenue
San Jose, CA 95125
"Business-eBay"

Michael O'Neill
P.O. Box 2900
Honolulu, HI 96846
"Business-(CEO) Pacific Century Financial"

Dwight D. Opperman
1601 - 2nd Avenue #5200
Minneapolis, MN 55402
"Business-Publishing"

Millionaire Directory   2nd edition

David O'Reilly
575 Market Street
San Francisco, CA 94105
"Business-(CEO) Chevron"

James F. Orr
PO Box 1638
Cincinnati, OH 45202
"Business-(CEO) Convergys"

William A. Osborn
50 South LaSalle Street
Chicago, IL 60675
"Business-(CEO) Northern Trust"

Lanny Outlaw
12200 North Pecos Street
Denver, CO 80234
"Business-(CEO) Western Gas Resources"

Linda Pace
445 North Main Avenue
San Antonio, TX 78205
"Business-Inheritance, Salsa"

Chris Pacitti
701 N. Brazos St., Suite 1400
Austin, Texas 78701
"Business-Venture Capitalist"

Warren J. Packard
DFJ, 400 Seaport Court, Suite 250
Redwood City, CA 94063
"Business-Venture Capitalist"

Dan Palmer
2525 Horizon Lake Drive
Memphis, TN 38133
"Business-(CEO) Concord EFS"

Mark Papa
1200 Smith Street
Houston, TX 77002
"Business-(CEO) EOG Resources"

Michael Parker
2030 Dow Center
Midland, MI 48674
"Business-(CEO) Dow Chemical"

Naser Partovi
2223 Avenida de la Playa, Suite 300
La Jolla, CA 92037
"Business-Venture Capitalist"

Kenneth Pasternak
525 Washington Blvd.
Jersey City, NJ 07310
"Business-(CEO) Knight Trading Group"

Piyush Patel
35 Industrial Way
Rochester, NH 03867
"Business-(CEO) Cabletron Systems"

Arthur Patterson
428 University Avenue
Palo Alto, CA 94301
"Business-Venture Capitalist"

Aubrey B. Patterson
One Mississippi Plaza
Tupelo, MS 38801
"Business-(CEO) BancorpSouth"

Henry M. Paulson, Jr.
85 Broad Street
New York, NY 10004
"Business-(CEO) Goldman Sachs"

Norman C. Payson
48 Monroe Turnpike
Trumbull, CT 06611
"Business-(CEO) Oxford Health Plans"

Millionaire Directory   2nd edition

Richard Taylor Peery
2560 Mission College Blvd. Suite 101
Santa Clara, CA 95054
"Business-Real Estate"

Nelson Peltz
280 Park Avenue
New York, NY 10017
"Business-Leveraged Buyouts"

Roger Penske
13400 Outer Drive West
Detroit, MI 48239
"Business-(CEO) United Auto Group"

Arno Penzias
2490 Sand Hill Road
Menlo Park, CA 94025
"Business-Venture Capitalist"

Andrew Jerrold Perelman
1999 Avenue of the Stars #3050
Los Angeles, CA 90067
"Business-Television"

Ronald Owen Perelman
625 Madison Avenue, 8th Floor
New York, NY 10022
"Business-Investments"

A. Jerrold Perenchio
1999 Avenue of the Stars
Los Angeles, CA 90067
"Business-(CEO) Univision Communications"

Angel Alvarez Perez
P.O. Box 9146
San Juan, PR 00908
"Business-(CEO) First BanCorp"

George Perlegos
2325 Orchard Parkway
San Jose, CA 95131
"Business-(CEO) Atmel"

H. Ross Perot
1700 Lakeside Square
Dallas, TX 75251
"Business-Investments"

Barry Perry
P.O. Box 770
Iselin, NJ 08830
"Business-(CEO) Engelhard"

Peter Pestillo
5500 Auto Club Drive
Dearborn, MI 48126
"Business-(CEO) Visteon"

Robert Einar Petersen
6420 Wilshire Blvd.
Los Angeles, CA 90048
"Business-Publishing"

Donald Peterson
211 Mount Airy Road
Basking Ridge, NJ 07920
"Business-CEO (Avaya)"

Robert L. Peterson
800 Stevens Point Drive
Dakota Dunes, SD 57049
"Business-CEO (IBP)"

Tom Peterson
2884 Sand Hill Road, Suite 121
Menlo Park, CA 94025
"Business-Venture Capitalist"

Howard Phanstiel
P.O. Box 25186
Santa Ana, CA 92799
"Business-(CEO) PacifiCare Health"

Michael Phippen
600-301 Blvd. West
Bradenton, FL 34205
"Business-(CEO) Staff Leasing"

Millionaire Directory   2nd edition

Joseph A. Pichler
1014 Vine Street
Cincinnati, OH 45202
"Business-(CEO) Kroger"

Mark C. Pigott
P.O. Box 1518
Bellevue, WA 98009
"Business-(CEO) Paccar"

Mark Pine
12657 Alcosta Blvd., Suite 190
San Ramon, CA 94583
"Business-Venture Capitalist"

Raymond Plank
2000 Post Oak Boulevard
Houston, TX 77056
"Business-(CEO) Apache"

William Podany
P.O. Box 19060
Green Bay, WI 54307
"Business-(CEO) ShopKo Stores"

Carl Pohlad
34 Kirby Puckett Place
Minneapolis, MN 55415
"Business-Banks & Sports Team"

Christian H. Poindexter
P.O. Box 1475
Baltimore, MD 21203
"Business-(CEO) Constellation Energy"

Kirk Pond
82 Running Hill Road
South Portland, ME 04106
"Business-(CEO) Fairchild Semiconduct"

Frederic M. Poses
P.O. Box 6820
Piscataway, NJ 08855
"Business-(CEO) American Standard"

Glen L. Post III
P.O. Box 4065
Monroe, LA 71211
"Business-(CEO) CenturyTel"

James Postl
P.O. Box 2967
Houston, TX 77252
"Business-(CEO) Pennzoil-Quaker State"

Kenneth Potashner
2841 Mission College Blvd.
Santa Clara, CA 95054
"Business-(CEO) SonicBlue"

Michael Potter
P.O. Box 28512
Columbus, OH 43228
"Business-(CEO) Consolidated Stores"

John Powell
2750 Sand Hill Rd.
Menlo Park, CA 94025
"Business-Venture Capitalist"

Michael F. Price
51 John F. Kennedy Parkway
Short Hills, NJ 07078
"Business-Money Management"

Larry L. Prince
2999 Circle 75 Parkway
Atlanta, GA 30339
"Business-(CEO) Genuine Parts"

Richard Priory
526 South Church Street
Charlotte, NC 28202
Business-(CEO) Duke Energy"

Robert Alan Pritzker
225 West Washington #1900
Chicago, IL 60606
"Business-Investments"

Millionaire Directory

2nd edition

Thomas J. Pritzker
200 West Madison, 39th Floor
Chicago, IL 60606
"Business-Investments"

Lawrence F. Probst III
209 Redwood Shores Parkway
Redwood City, CA 94065
"Business-(CEO) Electronic Arts"

Philip J. Purcell
1585 Broadway
New York, NY 10036
"Business-(CEO) Morgan Stanley Dean Witter"

David Pyott
P.O. Box 19534
Irvine, CA 92623
"Business- (CEO) Allergan"

Harry V. Quadracci
N63W230 Main Street
Sussex, WI 53089
"Business-Quad Graphics"

Frank Quattrone
c/o Credit Suisse First Boston
277 Park Avenue
New York, NY 10172
"Professional-Banker"

Gregory L. Quesnel
3240 Hillview Avenue
Palo Alto, CA 94304
"Business-(CEO) CNF"

Allen Questrom
6501 Legacy Drive
Plano, TX 75024
"Business-(CEO) J.C. Penney"

Andy Rachleff
2480 Sand Hill Rd., Suite 200
Menlo Park, CA 94025
"Business-Venture Capitalist"

Ernest Rady
23 Pasteur
Irvine, CA 92618
"Business-(CEO) Westcorp"

Vivek Ragavan
1310 Moffett Park Drive
Sunnyvale, CA 94089
"Business-(CEO) Redback Networks"

Franklin D. Raines
3900 Wisconsin Avenue NW
Washington, DC 20016
"Business-(CEO) Fannie Mae"

Richard Edward Rainwater
306 West 7th Street #1025
Fort Worth, TX 76102
"Business-Investments"

Mitchell Rales
1250 - 24th Street NW #800
Washington, DC 20037
"Business-Manufacturing"

Steven Rales
1250 - 24th Street NW #800
Washington, DC 20037
"Business-Manufacturing"

Theresia Gouw Ranzetta
428 University Avenue
Palo Alto, CA 94301
"Business-Venture Capitalist"

Millionaire Directory

2nd edition

Andy Rappaport
2480 Sand Hill Road, Suite 101
Menlo Park, CA 94025
"Business-Venture Capitalist"

Willam Rastetter
11011 Torreyana Road
San Diego, CA 92121
"Business-(CEO) IDEC Pharmaceuticals"

Naval Ravikant
2480 Sand Hill Road, Suite 101
Menlo Park, CA 94025
"Business-Venture Capitalist"

Lee Raymond
5959 Las Colinas Blvd.
Irving, TX 75039
"Business-(CEO) Exxon Mobil"

Steven A Raymund
5350 Tech Data Drive
Clearwater, FL 33760
"Business-(CEO) Tech Data"

Atiq Raza
3080 North First Street
San Jose, CA 95134
"Business-Venture Capitalist"

Tomo Razmilovic
One Symbol Plaza
Holtzville, NY 11742
"Business-(CEO) Symbol Technology"

N. Damodar Reddy
2575 Augustine Drive
Santa Clara, CA 95054
"Business-(CEO) Alliance Semiconductor"

Sumner Redstone
98 Balpate Road
Newton Centre, MA 02459
"Business- (CEO) Viacom"

Thomas L. Reece
280 Park Avenue
New York, NY 10017
"Business-(CEO) Dover"

Dennis H. Reilley
39 Old Ridgebury Road
Danbury, CT 06810
"Business-(CEO) Praxair"

Kevin P. Reilly, Jr
P.O. Box 66338
Baton Rouge, LA 70896
"Business-(CEO) Lamar Advertising"

Stan J. Reiss
Bay Colony Corporate Center
1000 Winter St., Suite 4500
Waltham, MA 02451
"Business-Venture Capitalist"

Eric G. Reiter
11150 Santa Monica Blvd. Suite 1200
Los Angeles, CA 90025
"Business-Venture Capitalist"

Glenn Renwick
6300 Wilson Mills Road
Mayfield Village, OH 44143
"Business-(CEO) Progressive"

Thomas Renyi
One Wall Street
New York, NY 10286
"Business-(CEO) Bank of New York"

Gregory L. Reyes
1745 Technology Drive
San Jose, CA 95110
"Business-(CEO) Brocade Communications"

Robert Edward Rich, Jr.
1150 Niagara Street
Buffalo, NY 14213
"Business-Rich Products Corp."

Millionaire Directory   2nd edition

Robert Edward Rich, Sr.
1150 Niagara Street
Buffalo, NY 14213
"Business-Rich Products Corp."

J. Joe Ricketts
4211 South 102nd Street
Omaha, NE 68127
"Business-Ameritrade"

David M. Rickey
6290 Sequence Drive
San Diego, CA 92121
"Business-(CEO) Applied Micro Circuits"

P. Anthony Ridder
50 West San Fernando Street
San Jose, CA 95113
"Business-(CEO) Knight Ridder"

Gary Rieschel
200 West Evelyn Ave., Suite 200
Mountain View, CA 94041
"Business-Venture Capitalist"

John J. Rigas
Main at Water Street
Coudersport, PA 16915
"Business-(CEO) Adelphia Communication"

Leonard Riggio
122 Fifth Avenue
New York, NY 10011
"Business-(CEO) Barnes & Noble"

H. John Riley, Jr
P.O. Box 4446
Houston, TX 77210
"Business-(CEO) Cooper Industries"

James A. Risinger
P.O. Box 718
Evansville, IN 47705
"Business-(CEO) Old National Bancorp"

Chris Risley
535 Middlefield Road, Suite 245
Menlo Park, CA 94025
"Business-Venture Capitalist"

C. Dowd Ritter
P.O. Box 11007
Birmingham, AL 35288
"Business-(CEO) AmSouth Bancorp"

Stephen D. Roath
P.O. Box 5222
Walnut Creek, CA 94596
"Business-(CEO) Longs Drug Stores"

Clifton S. Robbins
c/o General Atlantic Partners
Three Pickwick Plaza
Greenwich, CT 06830
"Business-Venture Capitalist"

James O. Robbins
1400 Lake Hearn Drive NE
Atlanta, GA 30319
"Business-(CEO) HJ Heinz"

Brian L. Roberts
1500 Market Street, 33rd Floor, East
Philadelphia, PA 19102
"Business-Cable Television"

Bryan Roberts
2494 Sand Hill Road, Suite 200
Menlo Park, CA 94025
"Business-Venture Capitalist"

George R. Roberts
9 West Street, 42nd Floor
New York, NY 10019
"Business-Leveraged Buyouts"

Leonard Roberts
100 Throckmorton Street
Fort Worth, TX 76102
"Business-(CEO) Radio Shack"

Millionaire Directory 2nd edition

Ralph Roberts
1500 Market Street
Philadelphia, PA 19102
"Business-(CEO) Comcast"

Jesse Mack Robinson
4370 Peachtree Road N.E.
Atlanta, GA 30319
"Business-Banking"

George A. Roche
100 East Pratt Street
Baltimore, MD 21202
"Business-(CEO) T. Rowe Price"

Arthur J. Rock
One Maritime Plaza #1220
San Francisco, CA 94111
"Business-Venture Capital"

Douglas Rock
16740 Hardy Street
Houston, TX 77032
"Business-(CEO) Smith International"

David Rockefeller, Sr.
30 Rockefeller Plaza, Room #5600
New York, NY 10112
"Business-Inheritance (Oil)"

Laurance Spelman Rockefeller
30 Rockefeller Plaza, Room #5600
New York, NY 10112
"Business-Inheritance (Oil)"

Winthrop Paul Rockefeller
The State Capitol
Little Rock, AR
"Business-Inheritance (Oil)"

T. J. Rodgers
3901 North First Street
San Jose, CA 95134
"Business-(CEO) Cypress Semiconductor"

Willem P. Roelandts
2100 Logic Drive
San Jose, CA 95124
Business-CEO (Xilinx)

Ernest C. Roessler
One Commerce Square
Memphis, TN 38150
"Business-(CEO) Natl' Commerce Bankcorp"

Steven R. Rogel
P.O. Box 2999
Tacoma, WA 98477
"Business-(CEO) Weyerhaeuser"

James E. Rogers
P.O. Box 960
Cincinnati, OH 45201
"Business-(CEO) Cinergy"

Bruce Rohde
One ConAgra Drive
Omaha, NE 68102
"Business-(CEO) ConAgra"

James Rohr
249 Fifth Avenue
Pittsburgh, PA 15222
"Business-(CEO) PNC Financial Services"

Philippe Rollier
12950 Worldgate Drive
Herndon, VA 20170
"Business-(CEO) Lafarge"

Michael Rolnick
305 Lytton Avenue
Palo Alto, California 94301
"Business-Venture Capitalist"

Richard Roscitt
12501 Whitewater Drive
Minnetonka, MN 55343
"Business-(CEO) ADC Telecom"

Millionaire Directory   2nd edition

Matthew Rose
2650 Lou Menk Drive
Fort Worth, TX 76131
"Business-(CEO) Burlington Santa Fe"

Robert E. Rose
777 North Eldridge Parkway
Houston, TX 77079
"Business-(CEO) Global Marine"

Benedict P. Rosen
P.O. Box 867
Myrtle Beach, SC 29578
"Business-(CEO) AVX"

Daniel D. Rosenthal
3501 Jamboree Road
Newport Beach, CA 9266
"Business-(CEO) Downey Financial"

Edward Roski, Jr.
P.O. Box 10
Inglewood, CA 90306
"Business-Real Estate & Sports Team"

Robert Rossiter
21557 Telegraph Road
Southfield, MI 48086
"Business-(CEO) Lear"

Michael I. Roth
1740 Broadway
New York, NY 10019
"Business-(CEO) MONY Group"

Ray Rothrock
2494 Sand Hill Road, Suite 200
Menlo Park, CA 94025
"Business-Venture Capitalist"

William J. Rouhana, Jr
685 Third Avenue
New York, NY 10017
"Business-(CEO) WinStar Communications"

John W. Rowe
151 Farmington Avenue
Hartford, CT 06156
"Business-(CEO) Aetna"

Allen R. Rowland
P.O. Box B
Jacksonville, FL 32203
"Business-(CEO) Winn-Dixie Stores"

Landon Rowland
920 Main Street
Kansas City, MO 64105
"Business-(CEO) Stilwell Financial"

Robert Rowling
420 Decker Drive #200
Irving, TX 75062
"Business-Oil & Gas"

Phillip Ruffin
1500 East 77th Street North
Wichita, KS 67147
"Business-Real Estate & Investments"

Gordon Russell
3000 Sand Hill Road
Bldg. 4, Suite 180
Menlo Park, CA 94025
"Business-Venture Capitalist"

Patricia F. Russo
600 Mountain Avenue
Murray Hill, NJ 07974
"Business-(CEO) Lucent Technologies"

Christopher Rust
3000 Sand Hill Road
Bldg. 4, Suite 180
Menlo Park, CA 94025
"Business-Venture Capitalist"

Millionaire Directory

2nd edition

John Rutherfurd, Jr
99 Church Street
New York, NY 10007
"Business-(CEO) Moody's"

Patrick George Ryan
c/o Aon Corp.
123 North Wacker Drive
Chicago, IL 60606
"Business-(CEO) Aon"

Thomas Ryan
One CVS Drive
Woonsocket, RI 02895
"Business-(CEO) CVS"

William J. Ryan
P.O. Box 9540
Portland, ME 04112
"Business-(CEO) Banknorth Group"

Thomas Ryder
Reader's Digest Road
Pleasantville, NY 10570
"Business-(CEO) Reader's Digest"

Haim Saban
c/o Fox Family Worldwide Inc.
10960 Wilshire Blvd.
Los Angeles, CA 90024
"Business-Medai (Cartoons)"

John Sall
SAS Campus Drive
Cary, NC 27513
"Business-Software"

Henry Samueli
P.O. Box 57013
Irvine, CA 92619
"Business-Broadcom"

Walter J. Sanders III
P.O. Box 3453
Sunnyvale, CA 94088
"Business-(CEO) Advanced Micro"

Wayne R. Sanders
P.O. Box 619100
Dallas, TX 75261
"Business-(CEO) Kimberly-Clark"

Marion O. Sandler
1901 Harrison Street
Oakland, CA 94612
"Business-(CEO) Golden West Financial"

Stephen W. Sanger
P.O. Box 1113
Minneapolis, MN 55440
"Business-(CEO) Caremark Rx"

Steve Sanghi
2355 West Chandler Blvd.
Chandler, AZ 85224
"Business-(CEO) Microchip Technology"

Roger W. Sant
1001 North 19th Street
Arlington, VA 22209
"Business-Energy"

A. Eugene Sapp, Jr
2101 West Clinton Avenue
Huntsville, AL 35805
"Business-(CEO) SCI Systems"

Paul Sarvadi
19001 Crescent Springs Drive
Kingwood, TX 77339
"Business-(CEO) Administaff"

Shirish S. Sathaye
2500 Sand Hill Road, Suite 200
Menlo Park, CA 94025
"Business-Venture Capitalist"

Millionaire Directory   2nd edition

Philip G. Satre
5100 West Sahara Avenue
Las Vegas, NV 89146
"Business-(CEO) Harrah's Entertainment"

Bernard Francis Saul II
One Quincy Street
Chevy Chase, MD 20815
"Business-Banking"

Mark Saul
70 Willow Rd, Suite 200
Menlo Park, CA 94025
"Business-Venture Capitalist"

William Savoy
110 - 100th Avenue NE, Suite 550
Bellevue, WA 98004
"Business-Venture Capitalist"

Richard Mellon Scaife
301 Grant Street #3900
Pittsburgh, PA 15219
"Business-Inheritance"

George A. Schaefer Jr
38 Fountain Square Plaza
Cincinnati, OH 45263
"Business-(CEO) Fifth Third Bancorp"

Leonard D. Schaeffer
1 WellPoint Way
Thousand Oaks, CA 91362
"Business-(CEO) WellPoint Health"

Chris Schaepe
2882 Sand Hill Road, Suite 106
Menlo Park, CA 94025
"Business-Venture Capitalist"

Bay Colony Corporate Center
1000 Winter St., Suite 4500
Waltham, MA 02451
"Business-Venture Capitalist"

John J. Schiff, Jr
P.O. Box 145496
Cincinnati, OH 45250
"Business-(CEO) Cincinnati Financial"

Andrew J. Schindler
P.O. Box 2866
Winston-Salem, NC 27102
"Business-(CEO) RJ Reynolds Tobacco"

Robert Schjerven
2140 Lake Park Blvd.
Richardson, TX 75080
"Business-(CEO) Lennon International"

Donald J. Schneider
P.O. Box 2545
Green Bay, WI 54306
"Business-Trucking"

Gene W. Schneider
4643 South Ulster Street
Denver, CO 80237
"Business-(CEO) UnitedGlobalCom"

Joe Schoendorf
428 University Avenue
Palo Alto, CA 94301
"Business-Venture Capitalist"

Nancy Schoendorf
2775 Sand Hill Road, Suite 240
Menlo Park, CA 94025
"Business-Venture Capitalist"

William Schrader
44983 Knoll Square
Ashburn, VA 20147
"Business-(CEO) PSINet"

Kenneth L. Schroeder
160 Rio Robles
San Jose, CA 95134
"Business-(CEO) KLA - Tencor"

Millionaire Directory　　　　　　　　　　2nd edition

John T. Schuessler
P.O. Box 256
Dublin, OH 43017
"Business-(CEO) Wendy's International"

Mike Schuh
70 Willow Rd, Suite 200
Menlo Park, CA 94025
"Business-Venture Capitalist"

Richard M. Schulze
7075 Flying Cloud Drive
Eden Prairie, MN 55344
"Business-(CEO) Best Buy"

Allan L. Schuman
370 North Wabasha Street
St Paul, MN 55102
"Business- (CEO) Ecolab"

Charles Schwab
101 Montgomery Street
San Francisco, CA 94104
"Business-Charles Schwab"

David C. Schwab
3000 Sand Hill Road,
Building 4, Suite 240
Menlo Park, CA 94025
"Business-Venture Capitalist"

Bernard L. Schwartz
600 Third Avenue
New York, NY 10016
"Business-(CEO) Loral Space & Commun"

Stratton Sclavos
1350 Charleston Road
Mountain View, CA 94043
"Business-(CEO) Verisign"

H. Lee Scott, Jr
702 Southwest 8th Street
Bentonville, AR 72716
"Business-(CEO) Wal-Mart Stores"

Walter Scott, Jr.
1025 Eldorado Blvd.
Broomfield, CO 80021
"Business-Telecom"

Francis Scricco
25 Hub Drive
Melville, NY 11747
"Business-(CEO) Arrow Electronics"

Richard M. Scrushy
One HealthSouth Parkway
Birmingham, AL 35243
"Business-(CEO) HealthSouth"

Brooke Seawell
575 High St., Suite. 400
Palo Alto, CA 94301
"Business-Venture Capitalist"

Terry Semel
3420 Central Expressway
Santa Clara, CA 95051
"Business-(CEO) Yahoo!"

Drew Senyei, M.D.
2223 Avenida de la Playa, Suite 300
La Jolla, CA 92037
"Business-Venture Capitalist"

Matthew Serra
112 West 34th Street
New York, NY 10120
"Business-(CEO) Venator Group"

Adam Sewell
305 Lytton Avenue
Palo Alto, California 94301
"Business-Venture Capitalist"

Cecil W. Sewell, Jr
P.O. Box 1220
Rocky Mount, NC 27802
"Business-(CEO) Centura Banks"

Millionaire Directory 2nd edition

Bobby S. Shackouls
P.O. Box 4239
Houston, TX 77210
"Business-(CEO) Burlington Resources"

Venu Shamapant
701 N. Brazos St., Suite 1400
Austin, Texas 78701
"Business-Venture Capitalist"

Richard Shapero
The Pioneer Hotel Building
2925 Woodside Road
Woodside, CA 94062
"Business-Venture Capitalist"

Kevin Sharer
One Amgen Center Drive
Thousand Oaks, CA 91320
"Business-(CEO) Amgen"

Scott Sheffield
5205 North O'Connor Blvd,
Irving, TX 75039
"Business-(CEO) Pioneer Natural Resourses"

Terry Shepherd
One Lillehei Plaza
St Paul, MN 55117
"Business-(CEO) St Jude Medical"

Michael Sheridan
1660 International Drive, Suite 400
McLean, Virginia 22102
"Business-Venture Capitalist"

Stephen Sherwin
342 Lakeside Drive
Foster City, CA 94404
"Business-(CEO) Cell Genesys"

Jon Shirley
One Microsoft Way
Redmond, WA 98052
"Business- Software (Microsoft)"

Walter Herbert Shorenstein
555 California Street #4900
San Francisco, CA 94104
"Business-Real Estate"

Patricia Short
401 West Mountain Avenue #200
Fort Collins, CO 80521
"Business-Hospital Equipment"

John Sidgmore
One Freedom Square
11951 Freedom Drive, Suite 1240
Reston, VA 20190
"Business-Venture Capitalist"

Jay S. Sidhu
P.O. Box 12646
Reading, PA 19612
"Business-(CEO) Sovereign Bancorp"

Sanjiv Sidhu
11701 Luna Road
Dallas, TX 75234
"Business-(CEO) i2 Technologies"

Thomas M. Siebel
2207 Bridgepoint
San Mateo, CA 94404
"Business-Siebel Syetem"

Herbert Siegel
767 - 5th Avenue, 46th Floor
New York, NY 10153
"Business-(CEO) BHC Communications"

Henry Silverman
9 West 57th Street
New York, NY 10019
"Business-(CEO) Cendant"

Harold Clark Simmons
5430 LBJ Freeway #1700
Dallas, TX 75240
"Business-Investments"

Millionaire Directory   2nd edition

Harris H. Simmons
1 South Main
Salt Lake City, UT 84111
"Business-(CEO) Zions Bancorp"

Melvin Simon
115 West Washington Street
Indianapolis, IN 46204
"Business- Shopping Center"

Charles Simonyi
One Microsoft Way
Redmond, WA 98052
"Business- Software (Microsoft)"

John R. Simplot
P.O. Box 27
Boise, ID 83707
"Business-Potatoes"

James D. Sinegal
999 Lake Drive
Issaquah, WA 98027
"Business-(CEO) Costco Wholesale"

David R. Skok
Bay Colony Corporate Center
1000 Winter St., Suite 4500
Waltham, MA 02451
"Business-Venture Capitalist"

Michael Small
3349 Route 138
Wall, NJ 07719
"Business-(CEO) Centennial Communications"

Bruce A. Smith
300 Concord Plaza Drive
San Antonio, TX 78216
"Business-(CEO) Tesoro Petroleum"

Dan F. Smith
P.O. Box 3646
Houston, TX 77253
"Business-(CEO) Lyondell Chemical"

Daniel E. Smith
150 Apollo Drive
Chelmsford, MA 01824
"Business-(CEO) Sycamore Networks"

Frederick Wallace Smith
942 South Shady Grove Road
Memphis, TN 38102
"Business-(CEO) FedEx"

James C. Smith
145 Bank Street
Waterbury, CT 06702
"Business-(CEO) Webster Financial"

Ollen Bruton Smith
P.O. Box 18747
Charlotte, NC 28218
"Business-(CEO) Sonic Automotive"

Orin Smith
P.O. Box 34067
Seattle, WA 98124
"Business-(CEO) Starbucks"

Robert Smith
27 Boylston Street
Chestnut Hill, MA 02467
"Business-(CEO) Neiman Marcus Group"

Steve Smith
950 Tower Lane, 18th Floor
Foster City, CA 94404
"Business-Venture Capitalist"

Vincent C. Smith
8001 Irvine Center Drive
Irvine, CA 92618
"Business- Software"

Millionaire Directory 2nd edition

Franchon M. Smithson
c/o General Atlantic Partners
Three Pickwick Plaza
Greenwich, CT 06830
"Business-Venture Capitalist"

John Snow
P.O. Box 85629
Richmond, VA 23285
"Business-(CEO) CSX"

John Albert Sobrato
10600 North De Anza Blvd. #200
Cupertino, CA 95014
"Business-Real Estate"

Jure Sola
2700 North First Street
San Jose, CA 95134
"Business-(CEO) Sanmina"

Howard Solomon
909 Third Avenue
New York, NY 10022
"Business-(CEO) Forest Labs"

Michael Solomon
2775 Sand Hill Road, Suite 240
Menlo Park, CA 94025
"Business-Venture Capitalist"

Theodore M. Solso
P.O. Box 3005
Columbus, IN 47202
"Business-(CEO) Cummins"

Rob L. Soni
83 Walnut Street
Wellesley Hills, MA 02481
"Business-Venture Capitalist"

Larry Sonsini
650 Page Mill Road
Palo Alto, CA 94304
"Professional-Lawyer"

James L. Sorenson, Jr.
1011 West 400 North
Logan, UT 84321
"Business-Technology"

James L. Sorenson, Sr.
1011 West 400 North
Logan, UT 84321
"Business-Technology"

George Soros
888 - 7th Avenue #3300
New York, NY 10106
"Business-Banking"

Clemmie Dixon Spangler, Jr.
P.O. Box 36007
Charlotte, NC 28236
"Business-Investments"

Alexander Gus Spanos
1341 West Robinson Drive #1A
Stockton, CA 95207
"Business-Real Estate"

John Sperling
4615 East Elwood Street
Phoenix, AZ 85040
"Business-(CEO) Apollo Group"

Steven Spielberg
P.O. Box 8520
Universal City, CA 91608
"Entertainment-Director, Producer"

David Spina
225 Franklin Street
Boston, MA 02110
"Business-(CEO) State Street"

Millionaire Directory   2nd edition

Steve Spurlock
2480 Sand Hill Rd., Suite 200
Menlo Park, CA 94025
"Business-Venture Capitalist"

John W. Stanton
3650 - 131st Avenue Southeast, #400
Belleview, WA 98006
"Business-(CEO) VoiceStream Wireless"

Rob Stavis
1865 Palmer Avenue, Suite 104
Larchmont, NY 10538
"Business-Venture Capitalist"

Andreas Stavropoulos
DFJ, 400 Seaport Court, Suite 250
Redwood City, CA 94063
"Business-Venture Capitalist"

Thomas G. Stemberg
500 Staples Drive
Framingham, MA 01702
"Business-(CEO) Staples"

William "Bill" Stensrud
2223 Avenida de la Playa, Suite 300
La Jolla, CA 92037
"Business-Venture Capitalist"

Thomas Stephenson
3000 Sand Hill Road
Bldg. 4, Suite 180
Menlo Park, CA 94025
"Business-Venture Capitalist"

Leonard Norman Stern
400 Plaza Drive #400
Secaucus, NY 07094
"Business-Real Estate"

Barry Sternlicht
777 Westchester Avenue
White Plains, NY 10604
"Business-(CEO) Starwood Hotels"

Mark Stevens
3000 Sand Hill Rd., Bldg. 4, Suite. 280
Menlo Park, CA 94025
"Business-Venture Capitalist"

J. W. Stewart
5500 NW Central Drive
Houston, TX 77092
"Business-(CEO) BJ Services"

Martha Stewart
19 Newton Toke #6
Westport, CT 06880
"Business-Media"

George J. Still, Jr.
525 University Avenue, Suite 800
Palo Alto, CA 94301
"Business-Venture Capitalist"

David A. Stonecipher
P.O. Box 21008
Greensboro, NC 27420
"Business-(CEO) Jefferson-Pilot"

Randy Strahan
2775 Sand Hill Road, Suite 240
Menlo Park, CA 94025
"Business-Venture Capitalist"

Erik Straser
2775 Sand Hill Road, Suite 240
Menlo Park, CA 94025
"Business-Venture Capitalist"

Jozef Straus
210 Baypointe Parkway
San Jose, CA 95134
"Business-(CEO) JDS Uniphase"

Stephen Straus
701 N. Brazos St., Suite 1400
Austin, Texas 78701
"Business-Venture Capitalist"

Millionaire Directory 2nd edition

David Strohm
2929 Campus Dr., Suite 400
San Mateo, CA 94403
"Business-Venture Capitalist"

Richard S. Strong
100 Heritage Reserve
Menomonee Falls, WI 53501
"Business-Money Management"

Neil Struminger
2750 Sand Hill Rd.
Menlo Park, CA 94025
"Business-Venture Capitalist"

Jon l. Stryker
303 North Rose Street #100
Kalamazoo, MI 49007
"Business-Stryker"

Ronda E. Stryker
2725 Fairfield Road
Kalamazoo, MI 49002
"Business-Stryker"

Donald L. Sturm
8390 East Crescent Parkway #300
Greenwood Village, CO 80111
"Business-Telecom"

Charles A. Sullivan
12 East Armour Blvd.
Kansas City, MO 64111
"Business-(CEO) Interstate Bakeries"

G. Craig Sullivan
1221 Broadway
Oakland, CA 94612
"Business-(CEO) Clorox"

Anthony Sun
2494 Sand Hill Road, Suite 200
Menlo Park, CA 94025
"Business-Venture Capitalist"

Judy Sundue
83 Walnut Street
Wellesley Hills, MA 02481
"Business-Venture Capitalist"

Robert Swanson, Jr
1630 McCarthy Boulevard
Milpitas, CA 95035
"Business-(CEO) Linear Technology"

Jim Swartz
428 University Avenue
Palo Alto, CA 94301
"Business-Venture Capitalist"

Gregory Swienton
3600 Northwest 82nd Avenue
Miami, FL 33166
"Business-(CEO) Ryder System"

Richard J. Swift
Perryville Corporate Park
Clinton, NJ 08809
"Business-(CEO) Foster Wheeler"

Richard F. Syron
P.O. Box 9046
Waltham, MA 02454
"Business-(CEO) Thermo Electron"

David Sze
2929 Campus Dr., Suite 400
San Mateo, CA 94403
"Business-Venture Capitalist"

Hisashi Tanaka
4100 Edison Lakes Parkway
Mishawaka, IN 46545
"Business-(CEO) National Steel"

Millionaire Directory   2nd edition

Jerome F Tatar
Courthouse Plaza Northeast
Dayton, OH 45463
"Business-(CEO) Mead"

Geoff Tate
4440 El Camino Real
Los Altos, CA 94022
"Business-(CEO) Rambus"

A. Alfred Taubman
200 East Long Lake Road #300
Bloomfield, MI 48303
"Business-Real Estate"

Sidney Taurel
Lilly Corporate Center
Indianapolis, IN 46285
"Business-CEO (Eli Lilly)"

Glen Taylor
1725 Roe Crest Drive
Mankato, MN 56003
"Business-Printing & Sport Team Owner"

Jack Crawford Taylor
600 Corporate Park Drive
St. Louis, MO 63105
"Business-Car Rental"

Jerry Taylor
2975 Stender Way
Santa Clara, CA 95054
"Business-(CEO) Integrated Device Tech."

Ron Taylor
2223 Avenida de la Playa, Suite 300
La Jolla, CA 92037
"Business-Venture Capitalist"

Joyce Raley Teel
500 West Capital Avenue West
Sacramento, CA 95605
"Business-Supermarkets"

Mark B. Templeton
6400 NW Sixth Way
Fort Lauderdale, FL 33309
"Business-(CEO) Citrix Systems"

Henri A. Termeer
One Kendall Square
Cambridge, MA 02139
"Business-(CEO) Genzyme-General"

David Thomas
200 Nyala Farms
Westport, CT 06880
"Business-(CEO) IMS Health"

G. Kennedy Thompson
One First Union Center
Charlotte, NC 28288
"Business-(CEO) First Union"

Carl F. Thorne
1445 Ross Avenue
Dallas, TX 75202-2792
"Business- (CEO) Ensco International"

Oakleigh Blackeman Thorne III
10200 East girard Avenue #A
Denver, CO 80231
"Business-Publishing"

John Thornton
701 N. Brazos St., Suite 1400
Austin, Texas 78701
"Business-Venture Capitalist"

Robert L Tillman
P.O. Box 1111
North Wilkesboro, NC 28659
"Business-(CEO) Lowe's Companies"

Glenn Tilton
2000 Westchester Avenue
White Plains, NY 10650
"Business-(CEO) Texaco"

Millionaire Directory   2nd edition

William B. Timmerman
1426 Main Street
Columbia, SC 29201
"Business-(CEO) Scana"

Ronald E. Timpe
1100 Southwest Sixth Avenue
Portland, OR 97204
"Business-(CEO) StanCorp Financial"

Tom Tinsley
c/o General Atlantic Partners
Three Pickwick Plaza
Greenwich, CT 06830
"Business-Venture Capitalist"

James S. Tisch
667 Madison Avenue
New York, NY 10021
"Business-(CEO) Loews"

Laurence Alan Tisch
Island Drive North
Manursing Island
Rey, NY 10021
"Business-Loews Corp."

Preston Robert Tisch
667 Madison Avenue, 7th Floor
New York, NY 10021
"Business-Loews Corp."

Lawrence Toal
589 Fifth Avenue
New York, NY 10017-1977
"Business-(CEO) Limited"

Barrett A. Toan
13900 Riverport Drive
Maryland Heights, MO 63043
"Business- (CEO) Express Scripts"

James R. Tobin
One Boston Scientific Place
Natick, MA 01760
"Business-(CEO) Boston Scientific"

Robert Toll
3103 Philmont Avenue
Huntingdon Valley, PA 19006
"Business-(CEO) Toll Brothers"

Louis Tomasetta
741 Calle Plano
Camarillo, CA 93012
"Business-(CEO) Vitesse Semiconductor"

Donald J. Tomnitz
1901 Ascension Boulevard
Arlington, TX 76006
"Business-(CEO) DR Horton"

Leonard Tow
3 High Ridge Park
Stamford, CT 06905
"Business- (CEO) Citzen Communications"

John M. Trani
1000 Stanley Drive
New Britain, CT 06053
"Business-(CEO) Stanley Works"

Kenny Troutt
8750 N. Central Expressway #2000
Dallas, TX 75231
"Business-Excell Communications"

Donald John Trump
721 Fifth Avenue
New York, NY 10022
"Business-Real Estate & Casinos"

Klaus Tschira
5555 Northeast Moore Court
Hillsboro, OR 97124
"Business-(CEO) Lattice Semiconductor"

Millionaire Directory   2nd edition

Marv Tseu
305 Lytton Avenue
Palo Alto, California 94301
"Business-Venture Capitalist"

Joseph M. Tucci
35 Parkwood Drive
Hopkinton, MA 01748
"Business-(CEO) EMC"

Cal Turner, Jr.
100 Mission Ridge
Goodlettsville, TN 37072
"Business-(CEO) Dollar General"

Lyle Turner
1600 Faraday Avenue
Carlbad, CA 92008
"Business-(CEO) Invitrogen"

Robert E. "Ted" Turner
1050 Techwood Drive NE
Atlanta, GA 30318
"Business-Media (CNN)"

Mike Tyrrell
One Canal Park, Suite 1120
Cambridge, MA 02142
"Business-Venture Capitalist"

John H. Tyson
P.O. Box 2020
Springdale, AR 72765
"Business-(CEO) Tyson Foods"

Steven Ferencz Udvar-Hazy
ILFC,
1999 Avenue of the Stars, 39th Floor
Los Angeles, CA 90067
"Business-Aircraft Leasing"

Albert Lee Ueltschi
c/o Marine Air Terminal
LaGuardi Airport
Flushing, NY 11371
"Business-Flight Safety"

Robert J. Ulrich
777 Nicollet Mall
Minneapolis, MN 55402
"Business-(CEO) Target"

Thomas Usher
600 Grant Street
Pittsburgh, PA 15219
"Business-(CEO) USX-US Steel"

Leslie Vadasz
2200 Mission College Blvd.
Santa Clara, CA 95052
"Business-Intel Capital"

Donald Valentine
3000 Sand Hill Road
Bldg. 4, Suite 180
Menlo Park, CA 94025
"Business-Venture Capitalist"

Roy Vallee
2211 South 47th Street
Phoenix, AZ 85034
"Business-(CEO) Avnet"

Jay Van Andel
7186 Windy Hill Drive S.E.
Grand Rapids, MI 49546
"Business-Amway"

Roland Van der Meer
305 Lytton Avenue
Palo Alto, California 94301
"Business-Venture Capitalist"

Millionaire Directory   2nd edition

Thomas Van Weelden
15880 N Greenway-Hayden Loop
Scottsdale, AZ 85260
"Business-(CEO) Allied Waste Industries"

Bay Colony Corporate Center
1000 Winter St., Suite 4500
Waltham, MA 02451
"Business-Venture Capitalist"

Mark A. Vershel
Bay Colony Corporate Center
1000 Winter St., Suite 4500
Waltham, MA 02451
"Business-Venture Capitalist"

Richard C. Vie
One East Wacker Drive
Chicago, IL 60601
"Business-(CEO) Unitrin"

Kenneth J. Virnig
718 University Avenue, Suite 110
Los Gatos, CA 95032
"Business-(CEO) Devine & Virnig"

Robert J. Vitito
328 South Saginaw Street
Flint, MI 48502
"Business-(CEO) Citizens Banking"

John Volk
428 University Avenue
Palo Alto, CA 94301
"Business-Venture Capitalist"

Michelangelo Volpi
170 W. Tasman Drive
San Jose, CA 95134
"Business-Cisco Systems, Inc"

Wesley W. Von Schack
P.O. Box 12904
Albany, NY 12212
"Business-(CEO) Energy East"

Joseph Vumbacco
5811 Pelican Bay Blvd.
Naples, FL 34108
"Business-(CEO) Health Management"

Todd Wagner
2914 Taylor Street
Dallas, TX 75226
"Business-Broadcast.com"

G Richard Wagoner, Jr
300 Renaissance Center
Detroit, MI 48265
"Business- (CEO) General Motors"

Norman Waitt
1125 South 103 Street #200
Omaha, NE 68124
"Business-(CEO) Waitt Media"

Theodore W. Waitt
4545 Towne Center Court
San Diego, CA 92121
"Business-(CEO) Gateway 2000"

John Walecka
3000 Sand Hill Rd., Bldg. 2, Suite 290
Menlo Park, CA 94025
"Business-Venture Capitalist"

David Walrod
1 Gorham Island
Westport, CT 06880
"Business-Venture Capitalist"

Millionaire Directory 2nd edition

Robert D. Walter
7000 Cardinal Place
Dublin, OH 43017
"Business-(CEO) Cardinal Place"

Alice L. Walton
10587 HWY. 281 South
Mineral Wells, TX 76067
"Business-Inheritance (Wal-Mart)"

Helen Walton
P.O. Box 2030
Bentonville, AR 72712
"Business-Inheritance (Wal-Mart)"

Jim Walton
201 N.E. "A" Streetß
Mineral Wells, TX 76067
"Business-Inheritance (Wal-Mart)"

S. Robson Walton
702 SW 8th Street
Bentonville, AR 72716
"Business-Executive (Wal-Mart)"

Robert L. Waltrip
P.O. Box 130548
Houston, TX 77219
"Business-(CEO) Service Corp International"

Richard L. Wambold
1900 West Field Court
Lake Forest, IL 60045
"Business-(CEO) Pactiv"

Charles B. Wang
One Computer Associates Plaza
Islandia, NY 11749
"Business-Computer Associates"

Jonathan Ward
One ServiceMaster Way
Downers Grove, IL 60515
"Business-(CEO) ServiceMaster"

Bruce D. Wardinski
6600 Rockledge Drive
Bethesda, MD 20817
"Business-(CEO) Crestline Capital"

Richard M. Wardrop, Jr
703 Curtis Street
Middletown, OH 45043-0001
"Business-(CEO) AK Steel Holding"

Daniel Warmenhoven
495 East Java Drive
Sunnyvale, CA 94089
"Business-(CEO) Network Appliance"

H. Ty Warner
280 Chestnut Avenue
Westmont, IL 60559
"Business-Beanie Babies"

Frederick J. Warren
11150 Santa Monica Blvd. Suite 1200
Los Angeles, CA 90025
"Business-Venture Capitalist"

Dennis Washington
101 International Way
Missoula, MT 59808
"Business-Conglomerate"

Larry Washow
1500 West Shure Drive
Arlington Heights, IL 60004
"Business-(CEO) Amcol International"

Charles L. Watson
1000 Louisiana Street
Houston, TX 77002
"Business-(CEO) Dynegy"

Noel G. Watson
P.O. Box 7084
Pasadena, CA 91109
"Business-(CEO) Jacobs Engineering"

Millionaire Directory   2nd edition

Craig E. Weatherup
One Pepsi Way
Somers, NY 10589
"Business-(CEO) Pepsi Bottling Group"

William S. Weaver
P.O. Box 97034
Bellevue, WA 98009
"Business-(CEO) Puget Energy"

Sanford Weill
153 East 53rd Street
New York, NY 10143
"Business-(CEO) Citigroup"

Arthur Weinbach
One Automatic Data Processing Blvd.
Roseland, NJ 07068
"Business-(CEO) Automatic Data"

Lawrence Weinbach
Unisys Way
Blue Bell, PA 19424
"Business-(CEO) Unisys"

John F. "Jack" Welch
3135 Easton Turnpike
Fairfield, CT 06431
"Business-(ex-CEO) General Electric"

Peter C. Wendell
3000 Sand Hill Rd., Building 4, Suite 240
Menlo Park, CA 94025
"Business-Venture Capitalist"

Gary Wendt
11825 N. Pennsylvania Street
Carmel, IN 46032
"Business-(CEO) Conseco"

Richard Wendt
P.O. Box 1329
Klamath Falls, OR 97601
"Business-Manufacturing & Resorts"

Norman H. Wesley
300 Tower Parkway
Lincolnshire, IL 60069
"Business-(CEO) Fortune Brands"

Blaine Wesner
701 N. Brazos St., Suite 1400
Austin, Texas 78701
"Business-Venture Capitalist"

Alfred P. West Jr.
1 Freedom Valley Drive
Oaks, PA 19456
"Business-(CEO) SEI Investments"

Lars Westerberg
3350 Airport Road
Ogden, UT 84405
"Business-(CEO) Autoliv"

David S. Wetherell
100 Brickstone Square
Andover, MA 01810
"Business-(CEO) CMGI, Venture Capitalist"

Leslie Herbert Wexner
P.O. Box 16000
Columbus, OH 43216
"Business-(CEO) Limited"

J. Steven Whisler
2600 North Central Avenue
Phoenix, AZ 85004
"Business-(CEO) Phelps Dodge"

Edward E. Whitacre, Jr.
175 East Houston
San Antonio, TX 78205
"Business-(CEO) SBC Communications"

Blair Whitaker
525 University Avenue, Suite 800
Palo Alto, CA 94301
"Business-Venture Capitalist"

Millionaire Directory   2nd edition

Dean White
1000 East 80th Place, #1600N
Merrillville, IN 46410
"Business-(CEO) Billboards"

Miles D. White
100 Abbott Park Road
Abbott Park, IL 60064
"Business-(CEO) Abbott Laboratories"

Tony White
761 Main Avenue
Norwalk, CT 06859
"Business-(CEO) Applera-Applied Biosys"

Roy Whitehead
425 Pike Street
Seattle, WA 98101
"Business-(CEO) Washington Federal"

Margaret C. Whitman
2145 Hamilton Avenue
San Jose, CA 95125
"Business-(CEO) eBay"

Mack Whittle, Jr
102 South Main Street
Greenville, SC 29601
"Business-(CEO) South Financial Group"

David R. Whitwam
2000 North M-63
Benton Harbor, MI 49022
"Business-(CEO) Whirlpool"

Michael W. Wickham
P.O. Box 471
Akron, OH 44309
"Business-(CEO) Roadway Express"

James B. Wigdale
770 North Water Street
Milwaukee, WI 53202
"Business-(CEO) Marshall & Ilsley"

Kenneth P. Wilcox
3003 Tasman Drive
Santa Clara, CA 95054
"Business-(CEO) Silicon Valley Bancshares"

Michael Wiley
P.O. Box 4740
Houston, TX 77210
"Business-(CEO) Baker Hughes"

Steven P. Williams
3000 Sand Hill Road,
Building 4, Suite 240
Menlo Park, CA 94025
"Business-Venture Capitalist"

Charles Williamson
2141 Rosecrans Avenue
El Segundo, CA 90245
"Business-(CEO) Unocal"

Robert G. Wilmers
One M & T Plaza
Buffalo, NY 14203
"Business-(CEO) M&T Bank"

Oprah Winfrey
P.O. Box 909715
Chicago, IL 60690
"Entertainment-Television"

Gary Winnick
360 North crescent Drive
Beverly Hills, CA 90210
"Business-Investments"

William Wise
P.O. Box 2511
Houston, TX 77252
"Business-(CEO) El Paso"

David C. Wittig
P.O. Box 889
Topeka, KS 66601
"Business-(CEO) Western Resources"

Millionaire Directory   2nd edition

David H. Wong
11150 Santa Monica Blvd. Suite 1200
Los Angeles, CA 90025
"Business-Venture Capitalist"

A. Greig Woodring
1370 Timberlake Manor Parkway
Chesterfield, MO 63017
"Business-(CEO) Reinsurance Group Am"

Wade Woodson
1600 El Camino Real, Suite 280
Menlo Park, CA 94025
"Business-Venture Capitalist"

John D. Wren
437 Madison Avenue
New York, NY 10022
"Business-(CEO) Omnicom Group"

Felix E. Wright
No 1-Leggett Road
Carthage, MO 64836
"Business-(CEO) Leggett & Platt"

Michael W. Wright
P.O. Box 990
Minneapolis, MN 55440
Business-CEO (Supervalu)

William Wrigley, Jr.
410 North Michigan Avenue
Chicago, IL 60611
"Business-Chewing Gum"

Perry Wu
305 Lytton Avenue
Palo Alto, California 94301
"Business-Venture Capitalist"

Samuel Wyly
P.O. Box 619566
Dallas, TX 75063
"Business-Investment"

Lior E. Yahalomi
3000 Alpine Road
Menlo Park, CA 94028
"Business-Venture Capitalist"

Geoff Yang
3000 Sand Hill Rd., Bldg. 2, Suite 290
Menlo Park, CA 94025
"Business-Venture Capitalist"

Jerry Yang
3420 Central Expressway
Santa Clara, CA 95051
"Business-Yahoo!"

Carl Yankowski
5470 Great America Parkway
Santa Clara, CA 95052
"Business-(CEO) Palm"

Alex Yemenidjian
2500 Broadway Street
Santa Monica, CA 90404
"Business-CEO (Metro-Goldwyn-Mayer)"

Charles R. Yoon
11150 Santa Monica Blvd. Suite 1200
Los Angeles, CA 90025
"Business-Venture Capitalist"

Larry D. Yost
2135 West Maple Road
Troy, MI 48084
"Business-(CEO) ArvinMeritor"

R. David Yost
1300 Morris Drive
Chesterbrook, PA 19087
"Business-(CEO) AmeriSource Health"

Millionaire Directory 2nd edition

Michael R. Young
P.O. Box 1592-364L
York, PA 17405
"Business-(CEO) York International"

William Younger
755 Page Mill Rd., Suite A-200
Palo Alto, CA 94304
"Business-Venture Capitalist"

Henry C. Yuen
135 North Robles Avenue #800
Pasadena, CA 91101
"Business-(CEO) Gemstar-TV Guide"

George Zachary
2775 Sand Hill Road, Suite 240
Menlo Park, CA 94025
"Business-Venture Capitalist"

Felix Zandman
63 Lincoln Highway
Malvern, PA 19355
"Business-(CEO) Vishay Intertech"

Ronald Zebeck
10900 Wayzata Blvd.
Minnetonka, MN 55305
"Business-CEO (Metris Companies)"

Ronald H. Zech
500 West Monroe Street
Chicago, IL 60661
"Business-(CEO) GATX"

Samuel Zell
2 North Riverside Plaza #2100
Chicago, IL 60606
"Business-(CEO) Citigroup"

Daniel Morton Ziff
153 East 53rd Street, 43rd floor
New York, NY 10122
"Business-Publishing"

Dirk Edward Ziff
153 East 53rd Street, 43rd floor
New York, NY 10122
"Business-Publishing"

Robert David Ziff
153 East 53rd Street, 43rd floor
New York, NY 10122
"Business-Publishing"

James Zimmerman
7 West Seventh Street
Cincinnati, OH 45202
"Business-(CEO) Federated Dept. Stores"

William D. Zollars
P.O. Box 7563
Overland Park, KS 66207
"Business-(CEO) Yellow"

A. C. Zucaro
307 North Michigan Avenue
Chicago, IL 60601
"Business-(CEO) Old Republic International"

Mortimer Benjamin Zuckerman
450 West 33rd Street, 3rd Floor
New York, NY 10001
"Business-Real Estate"

Bryan J. Zwan
15550 Lightwave Drive
Clearwater, FL 33760
"Business-Technology"

MAKE CONTACT WITH THE STARS!

The Celebrity Directory™ 2004-2005

covers the entire spectrum of celebrities. If a person is famous or worth locating, it's almost certain that their address can be found in here.
ISBN 0-943213-48-7

Only $39.95 + *$3.95 postage & handling*

The Venture Capitalists & Angel Inventors Directory™ (2nd Edition)

it's for anyone who is looking for money to start a business, buy a business or expand an existing business. It lists name, address, phone number and website of America's wealthiest inventors.
ISBN 0-943213-47-9

Only $21.95 + *$3.95 postage & handling*

The Celebrity Locator™ 2004-2005

The Celebrity Locator is our complete database for locating celebrities. If a person is famous and worth locating, it's almost certain that their regular address (almost 12,000) and website address can be found in here.
ISBN 0-943213-51-7

Only $79.95 + *$3.95 postage & handling*

The Millionaire Directory™ (2nd Edition)

lists name and address of thousands of millionaires & billionaires! It's the ultimate guide to identify and contact the rich in America!
ISBN 0-943213-46-0

Only $14.95 + *$3.00 postage & handling*

The 2004-2005 Star Guide™

is the most reliable and up-to-date guide available for over 3200 addresses of major stars from every field.
ISBN 0-943213-49-5

Only $14.95 + *$3.00 postage & handling*

Name _____

Address _____

City, State, Zip _____

___ Copies of **Celebrity Directory**™ @ $39.95 each + $3.95 P&H
___ Copies of **Star Guide**™ @ $14.95 + $3.00 P&H
___ Copies of **The Venture & Angel Inventors Directory**™ @ $21.95 each + $3.95 P&H
___ Copies of **The Millionaire Directory**™ @ $14.95 each + $3.00 P&H
___ Copies of **Celebrity Locator**™ @ $79.95 each + $3.95 P&H

Total Order $ _____,_____
(Add $3.90 per item for 2nd DAY PRIORITY MAIL)→Total Postage & Handling $ _____,_____
MI Residents add 6% Sales Tax* $ _____,_____
Total Enclosed $ _____,_____

Mail completed form to:

AIR
AXIOM INFORMATION RESOURCES

*Michigan Sales Tax:
Celebrity Directory - $2.40   Star Guide - $0.90
Millionaire Directory - $0.90   Celebrity Locator - $4.80
Venture Capitalists & Angel Investors Directory - $1.32